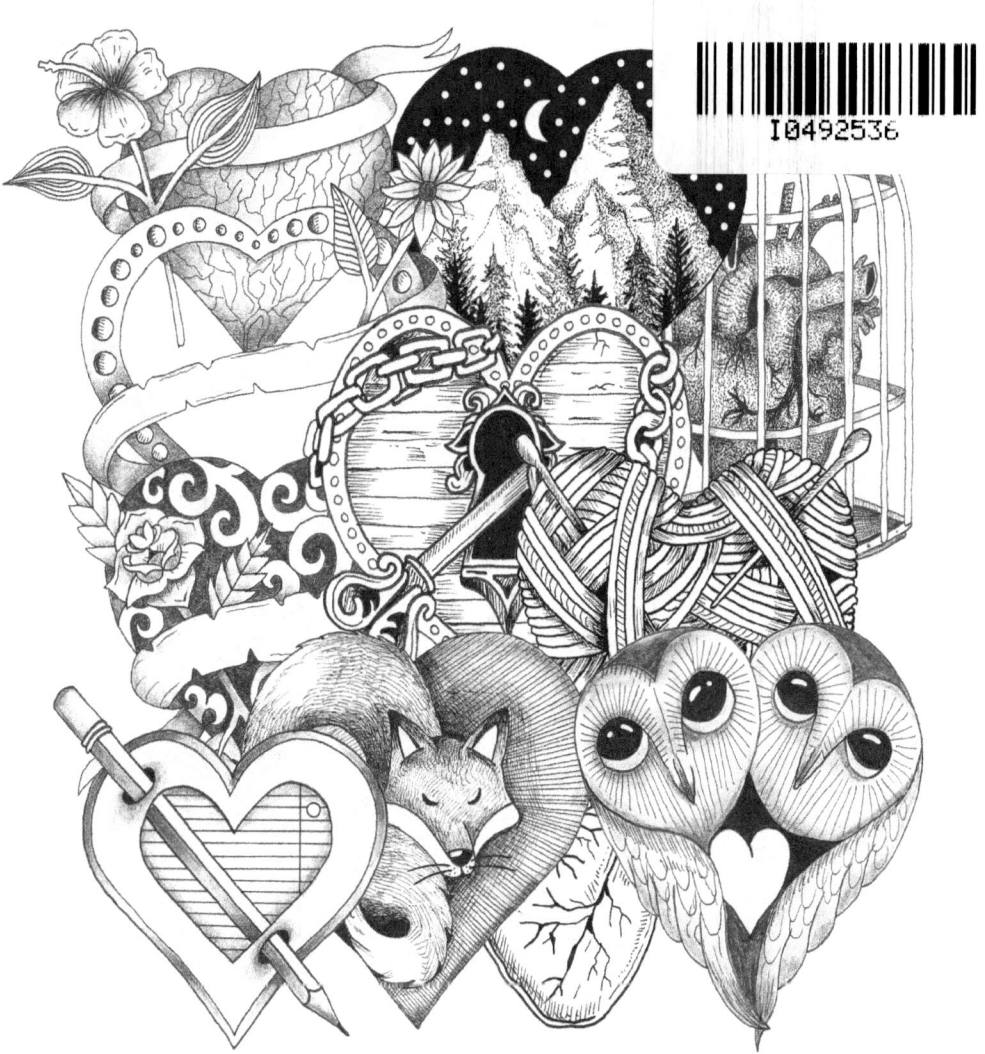

I0492536

Get ready for the most exciting collection of hand-drawn hearts ever!

Every single design in this book comes from the hand-drawn illustrations by best-selling coloring book creator Steve 'Squidoodle' Turner. From anatomical hearts, to animal hearts, traditional tattoo styles, futuristic steampunk mechanical hearts and so much more, there is something for everyone. Perfect for coloring, crafting and scrapbooking…. and of course, if you are considering a heart tattoo, you're sure to find a design inside this book!

A Hundred Hearts

Hand-drawn heart tattoos for coloring, crafting and scrapbooking.

Every single heart design in this book is © Squidoodle. You are free to get any design tattooed on yourself without permission from the author. You can also use the designs in craft projects, coloring and scrapbooking without permission but you cannot share the linework with others without prior permission from the author.

Copyright © 2018 Steve Turner (alias Squidoodle).
The rights of Steve Turner (Squidoodle) to be identified as the illustrator of this work has been asserted by him in accordance with the Copyright, Designs and Patents Act 1988.
All rights reserved, including the right of reproduction in whole or in any part in any form.

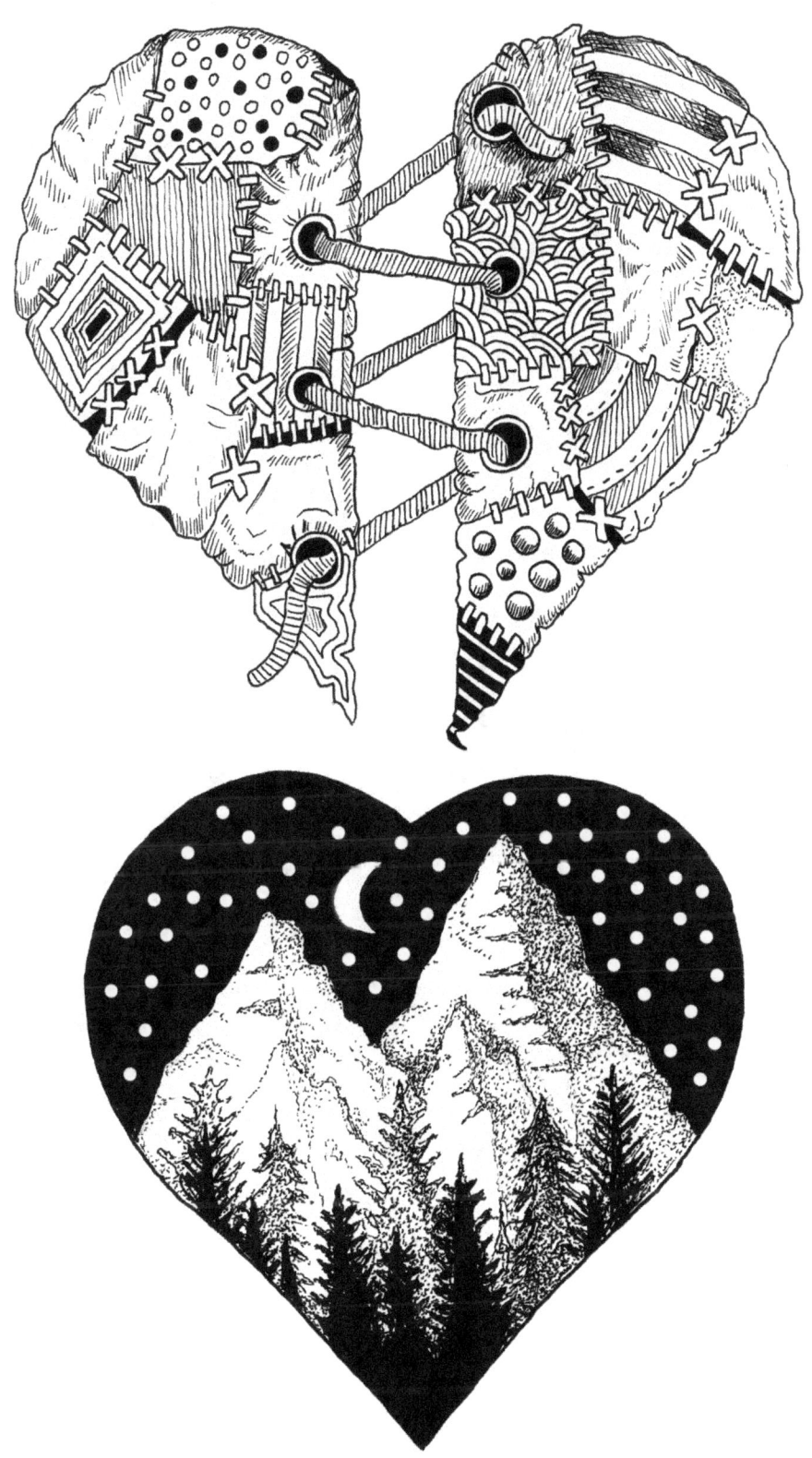

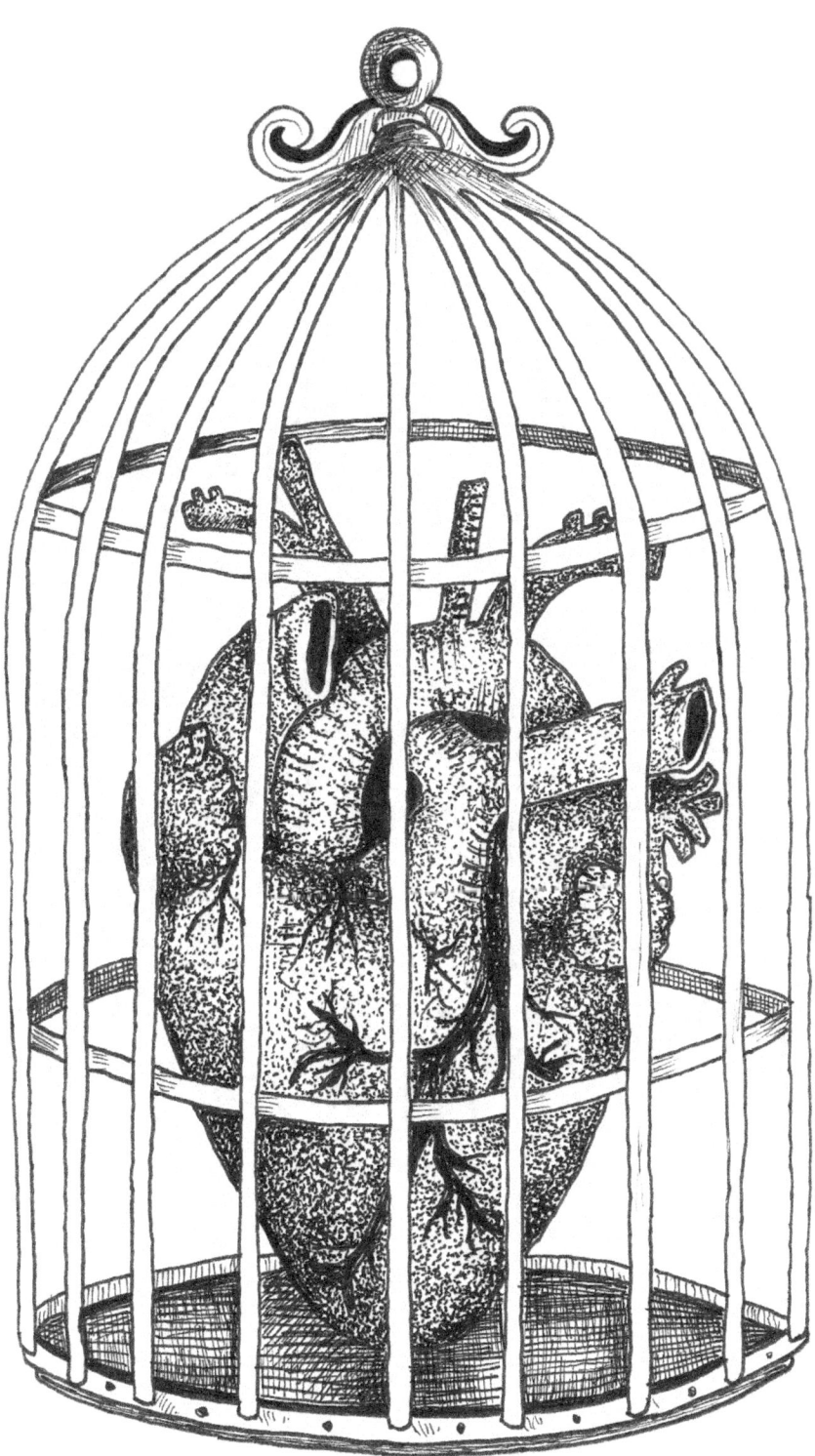

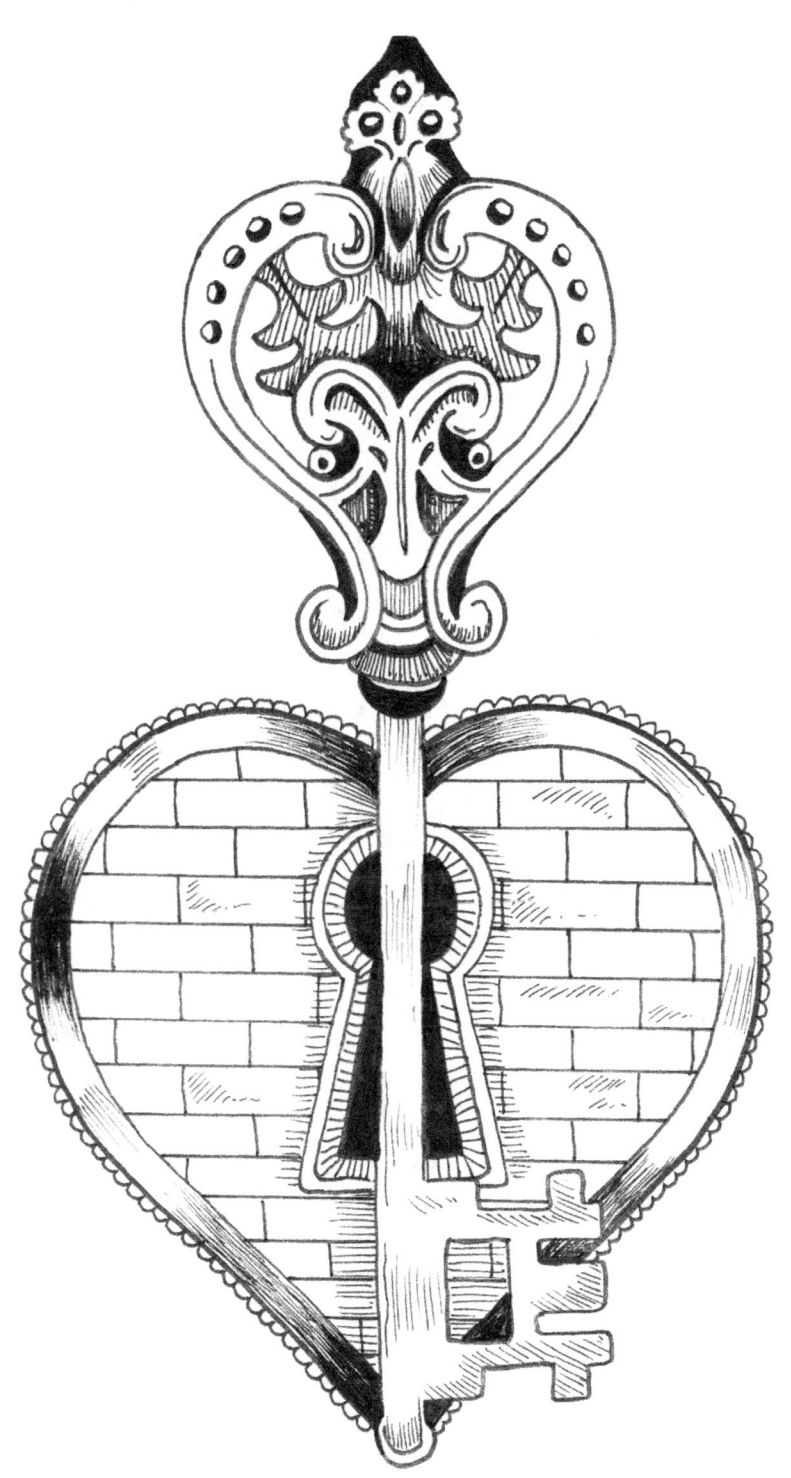

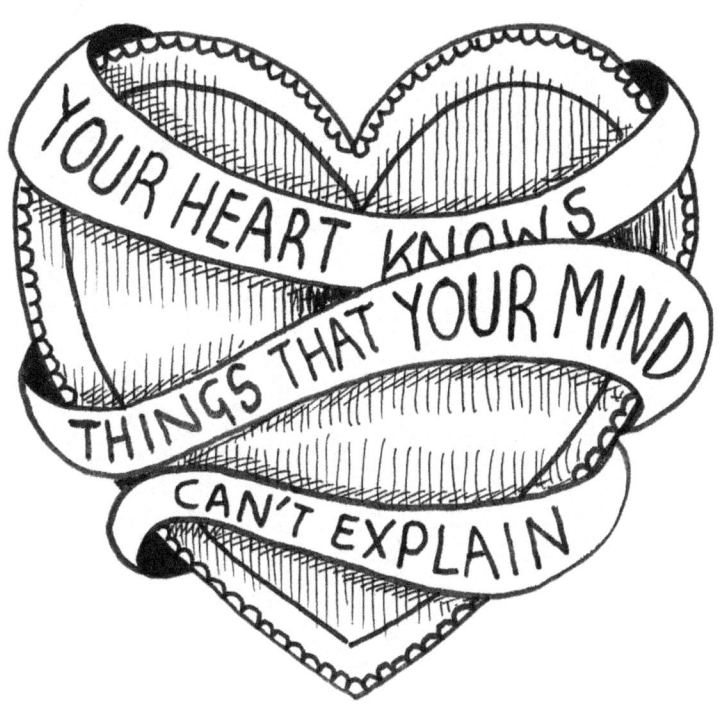

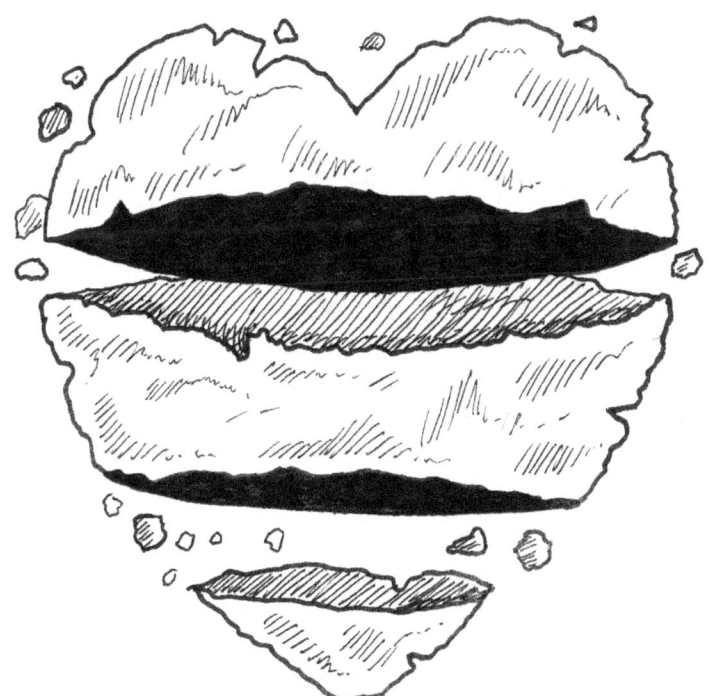

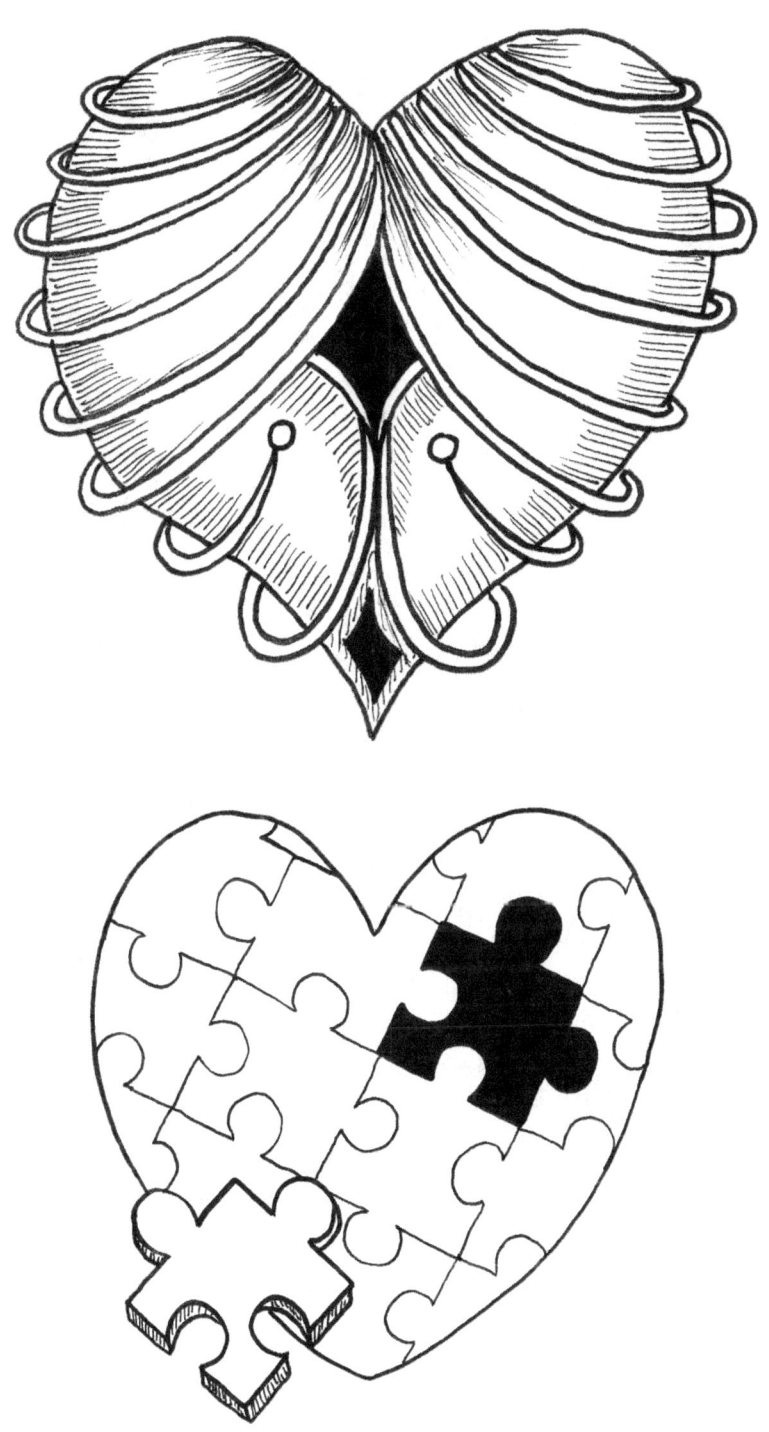

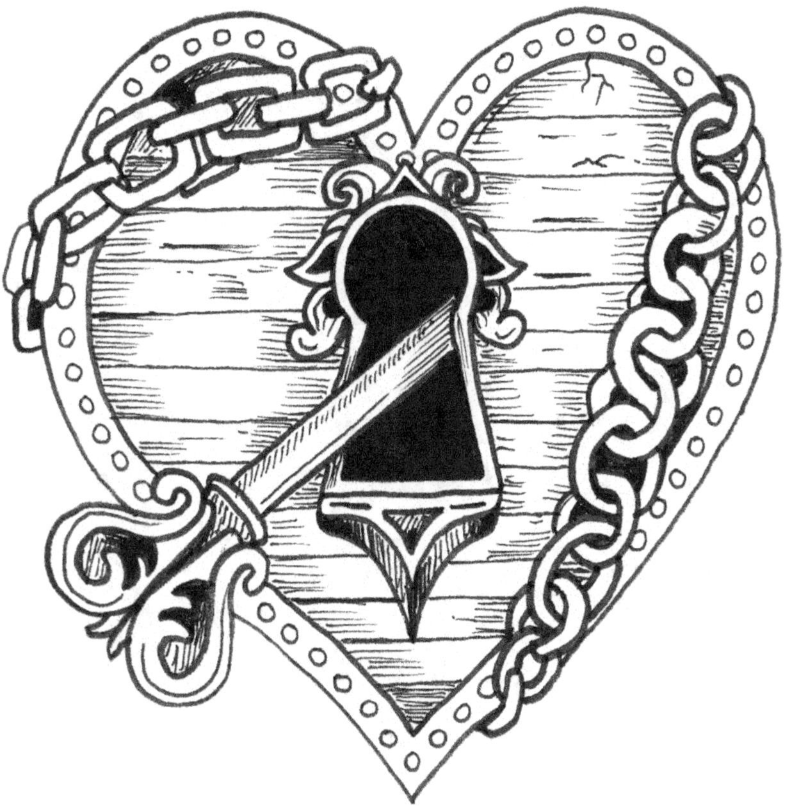

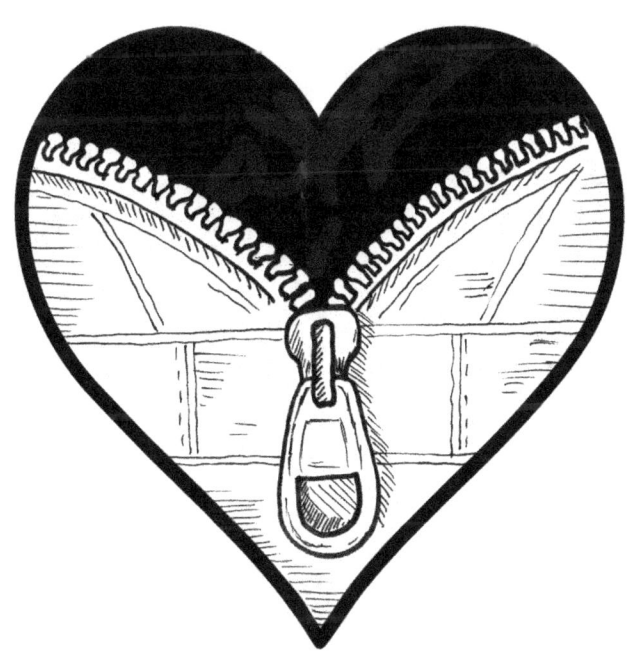

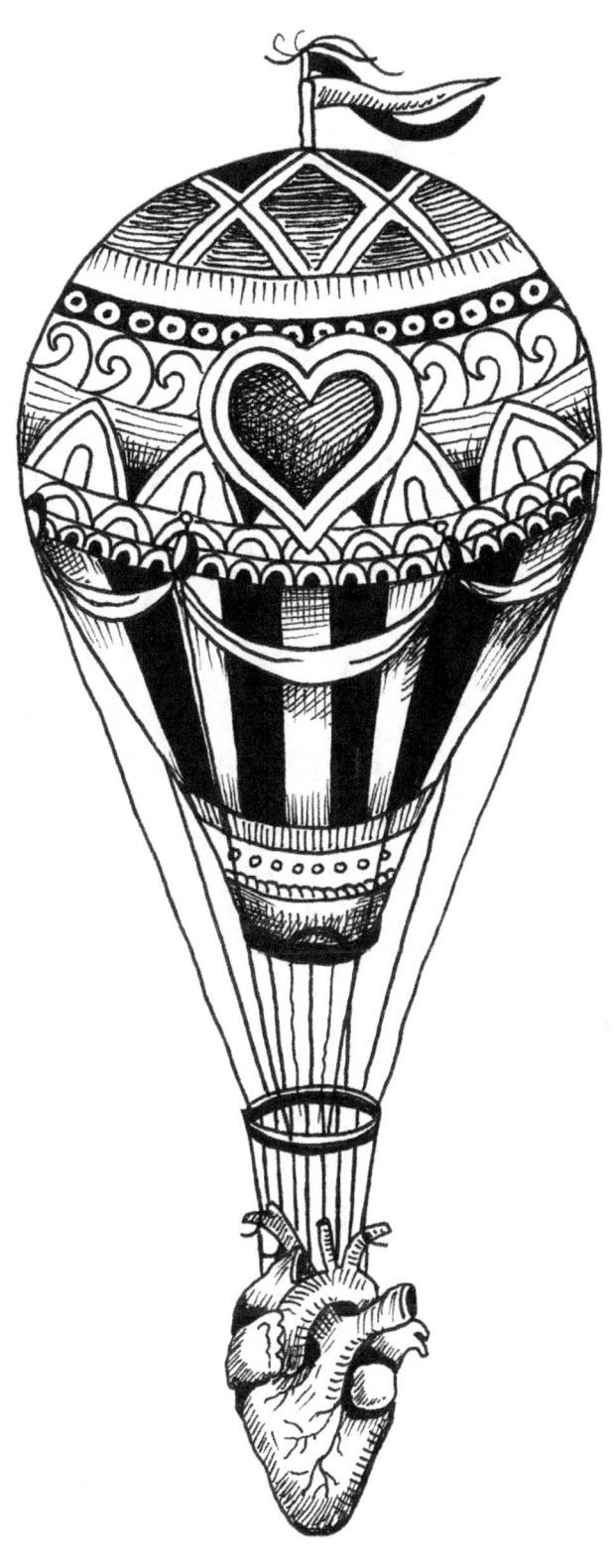

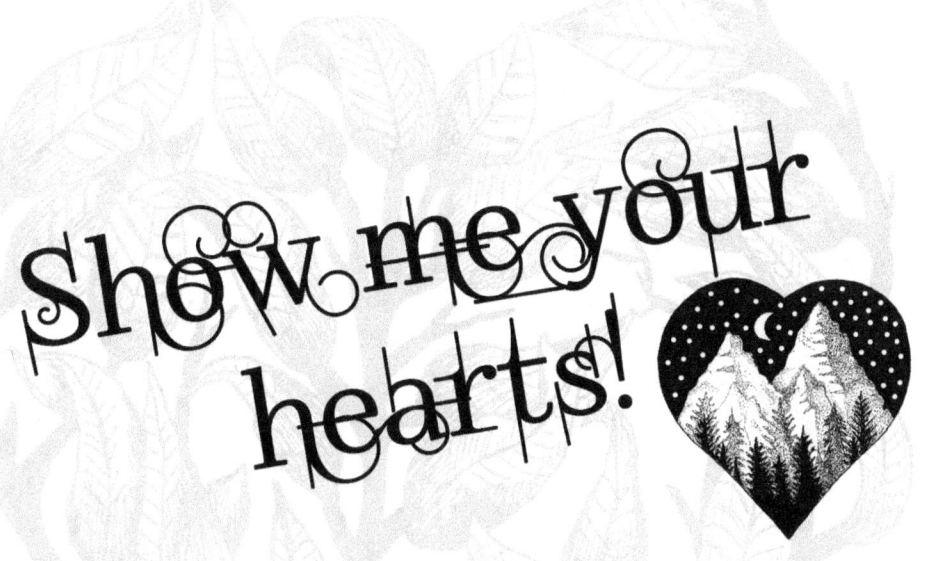

Show me your hearts!

I'd love to see what you do with the hearts in this book. Whether you color them, craft with them, make greetings cards, add them to projects, or even treat yourself to a heart tattoo for real!

 @squidoodleart

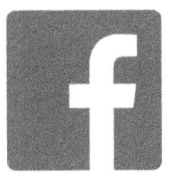 facebook.com/SquidDoodleArt

Make sure you follow me on instagram and facebook for regular giveaways and new book announcements!

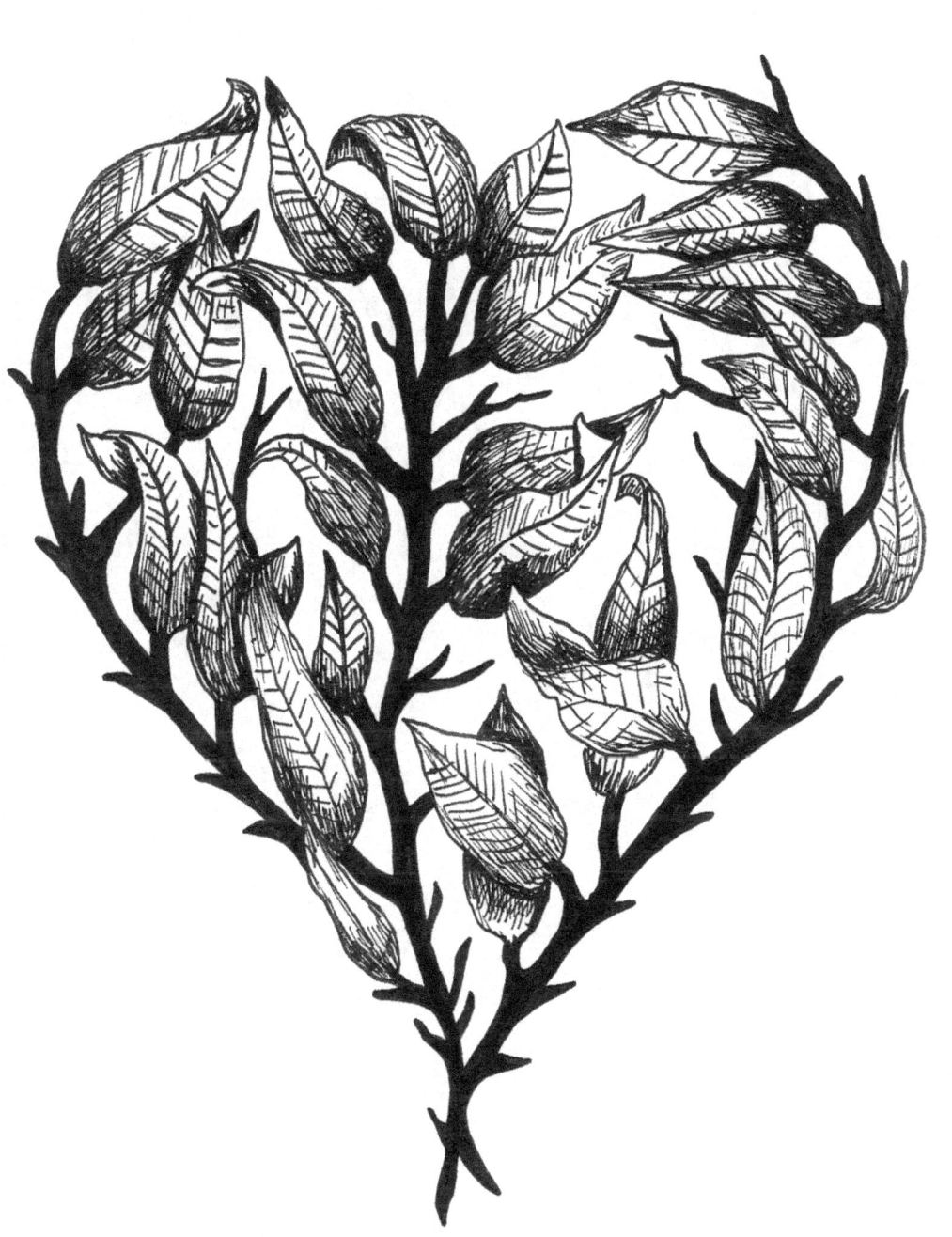

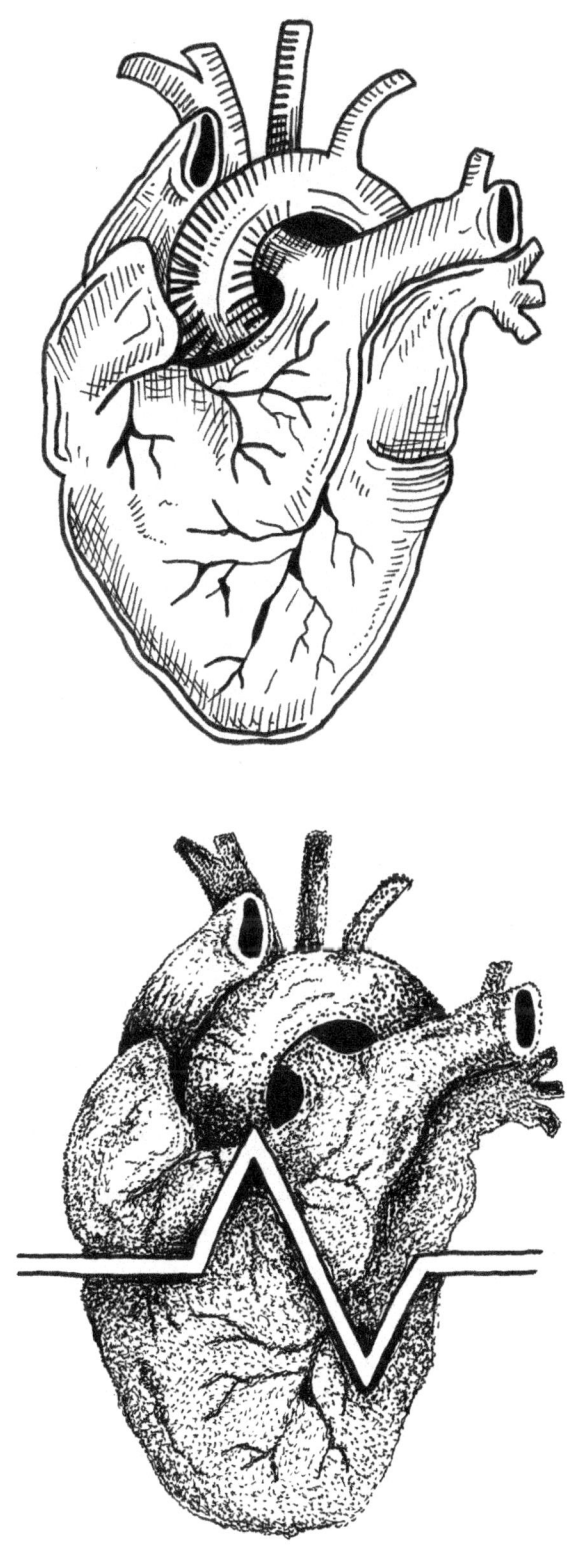

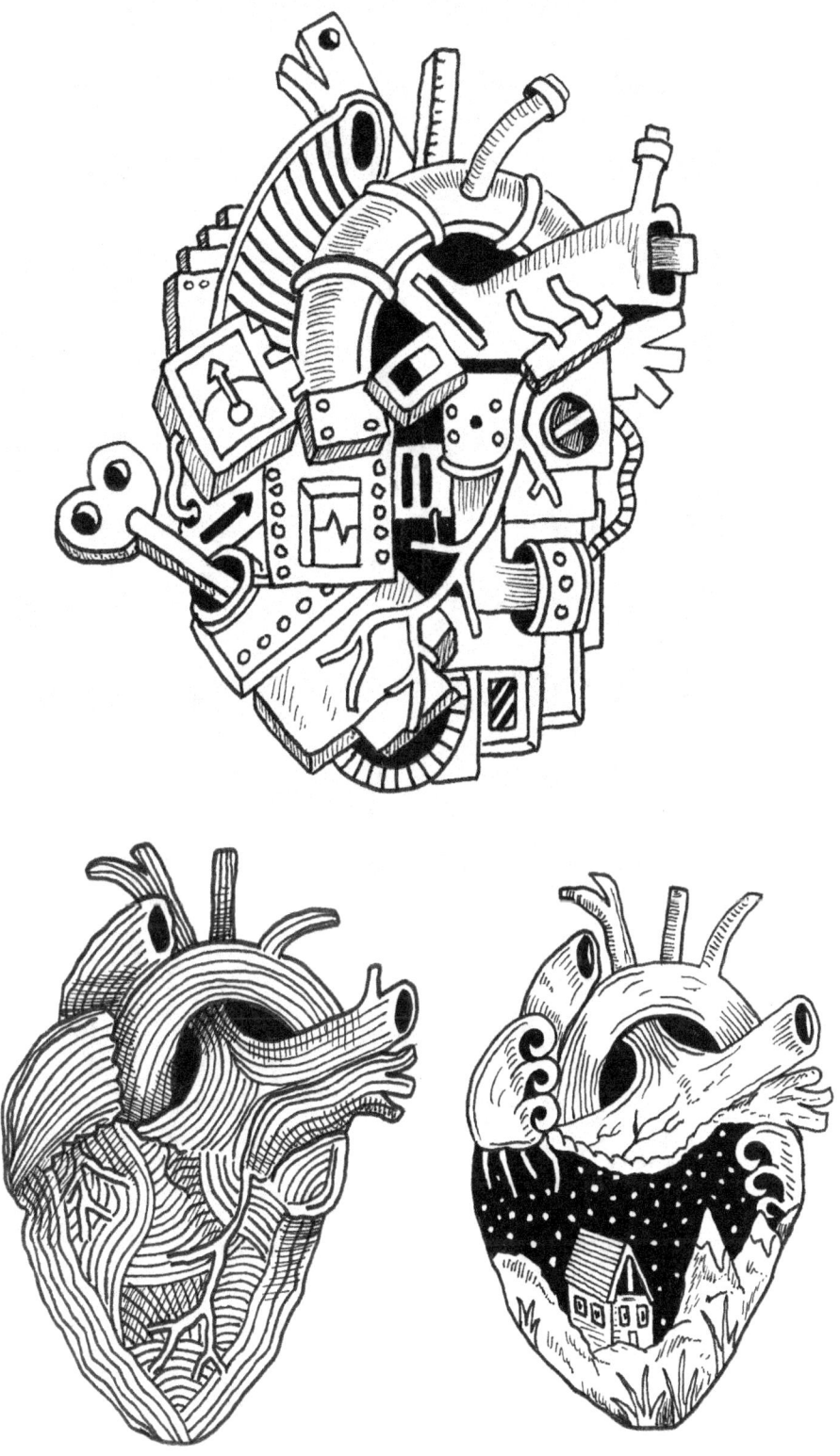

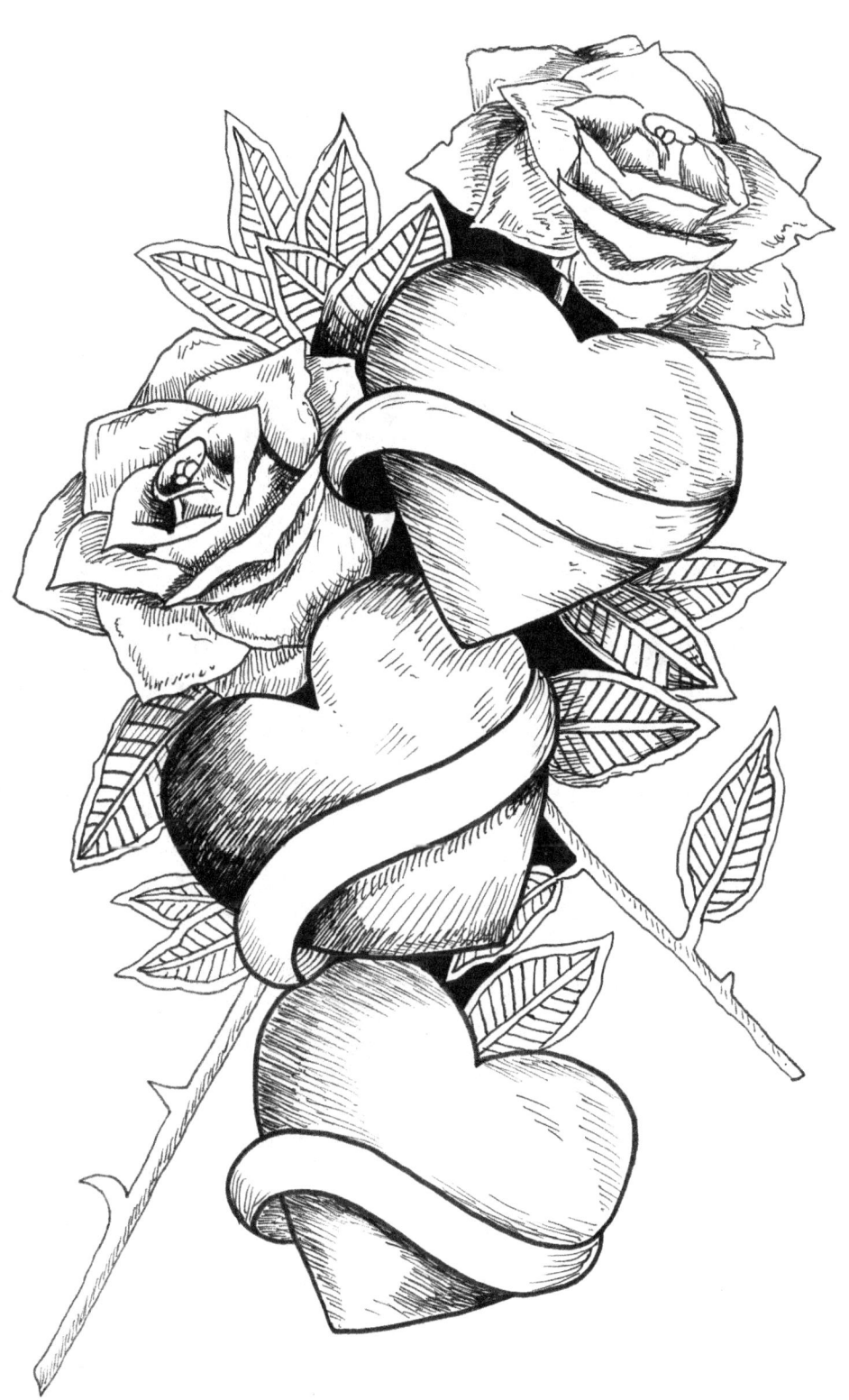

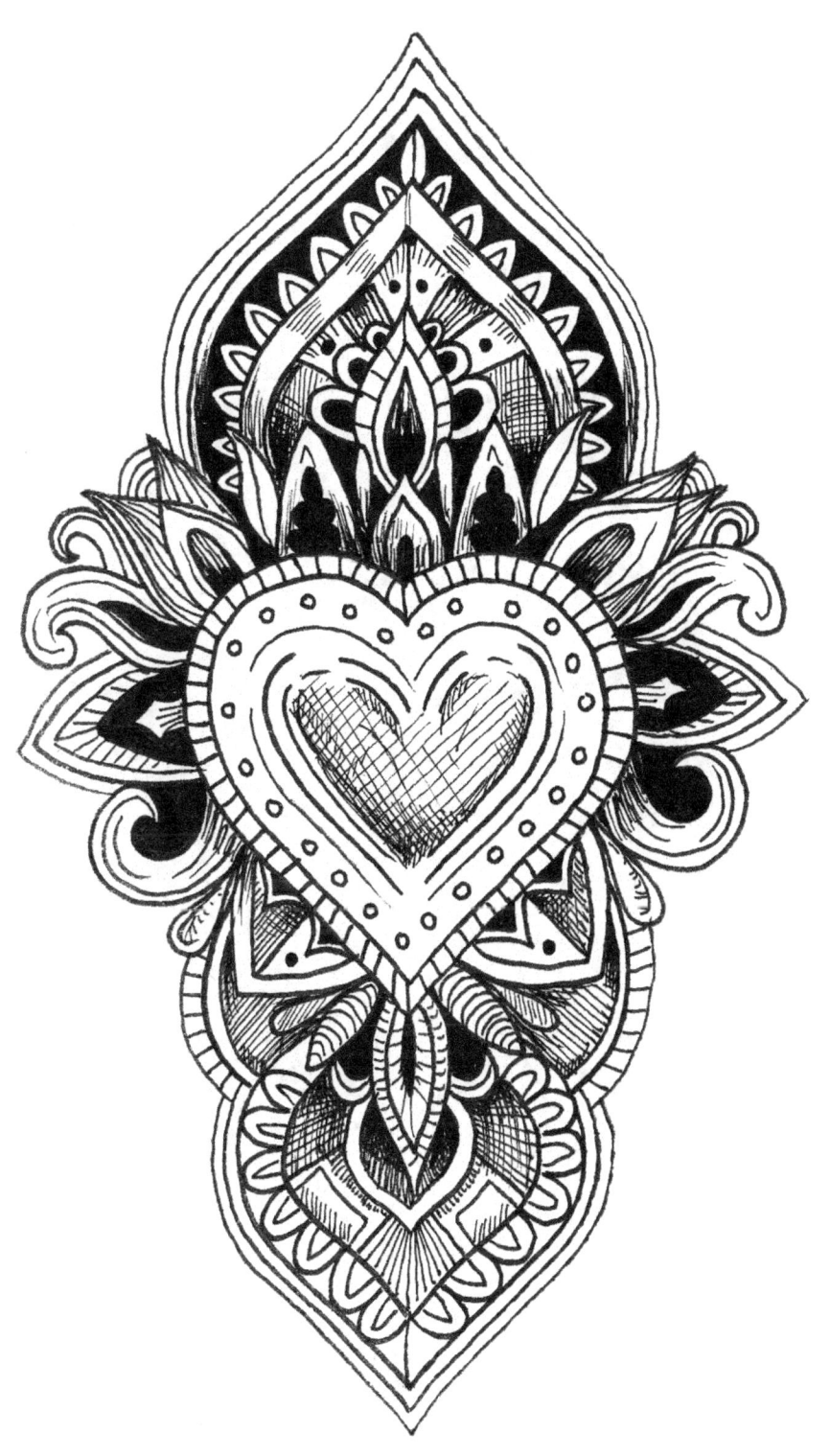

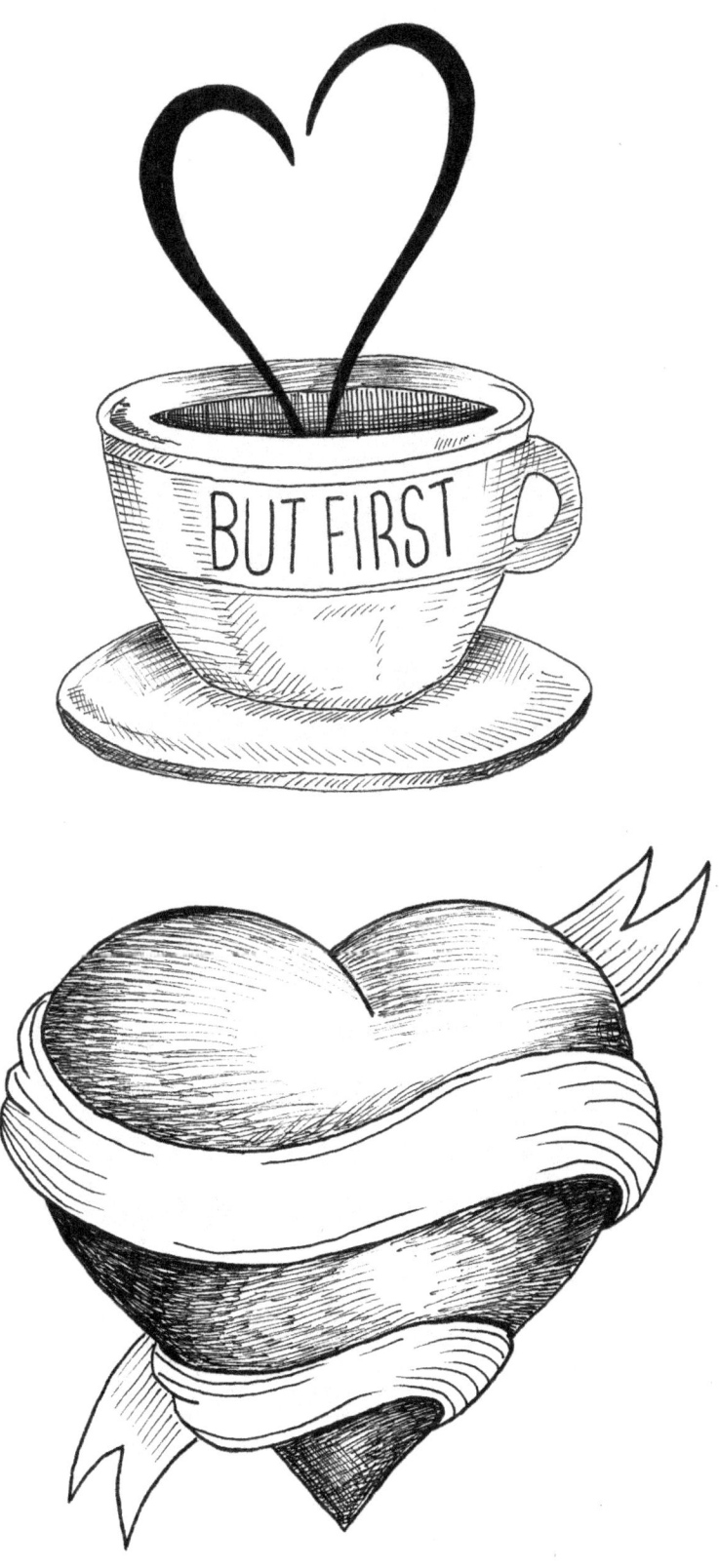

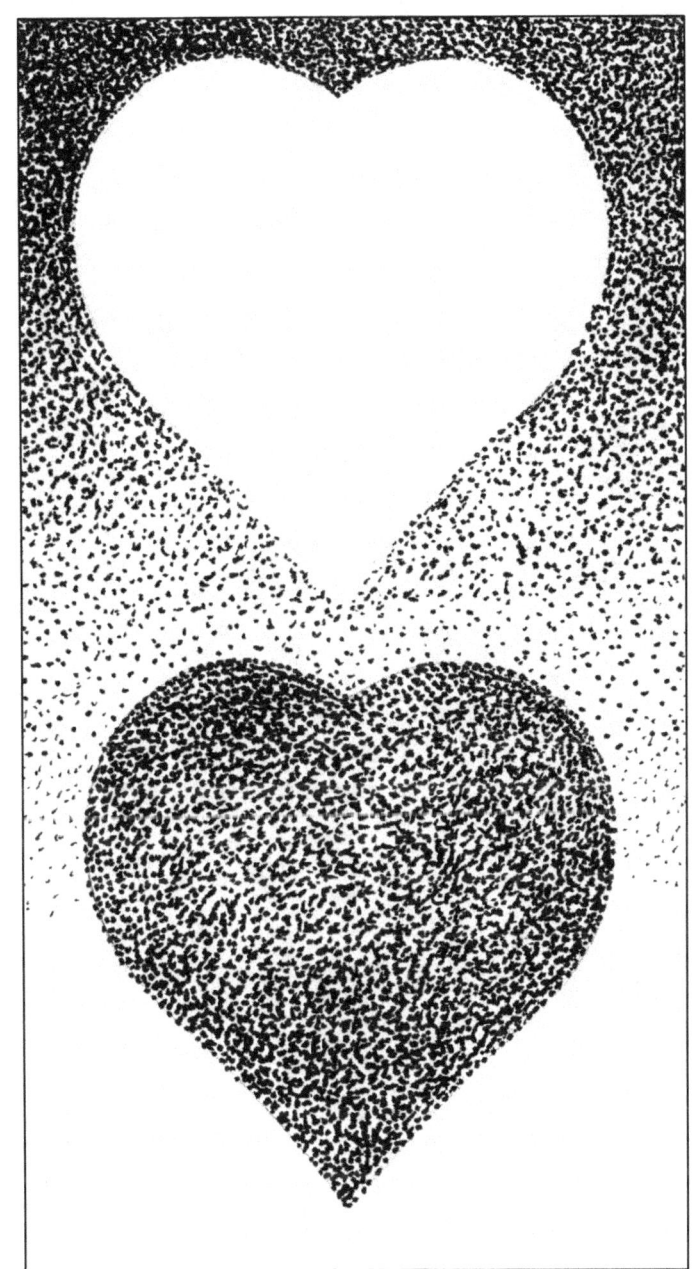

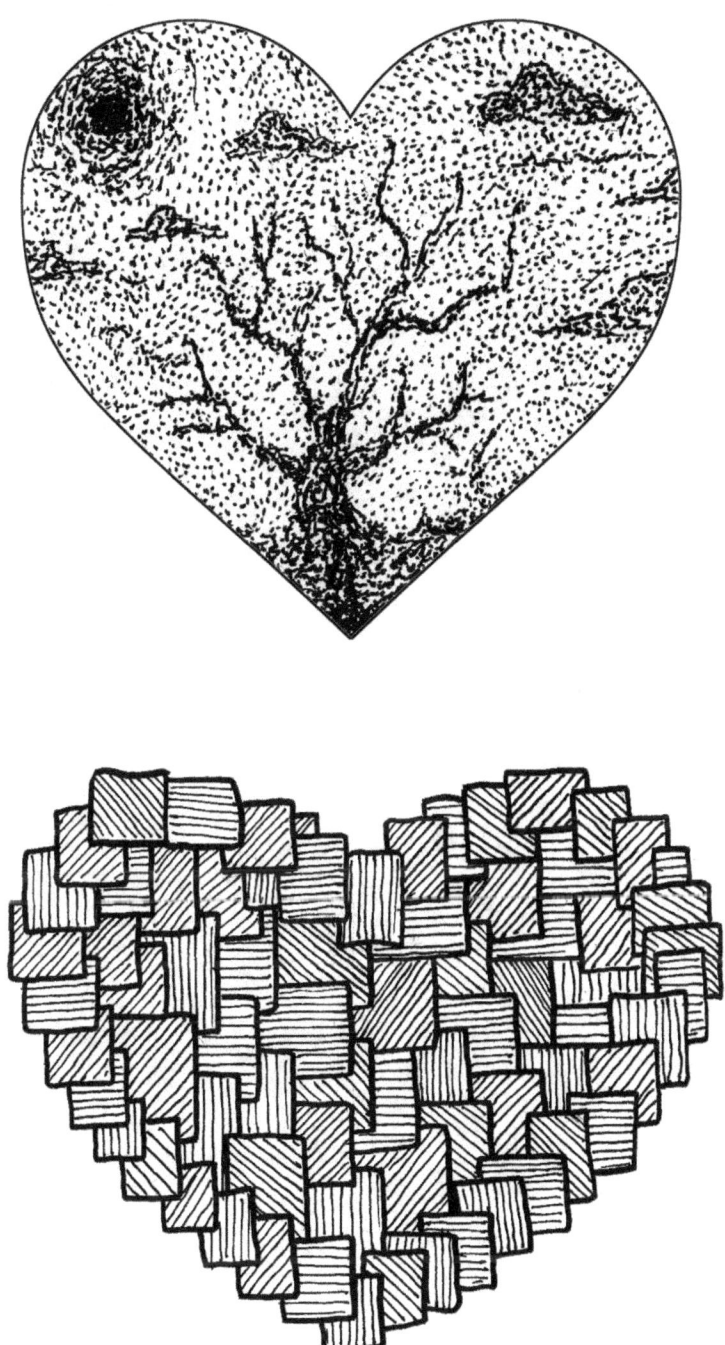

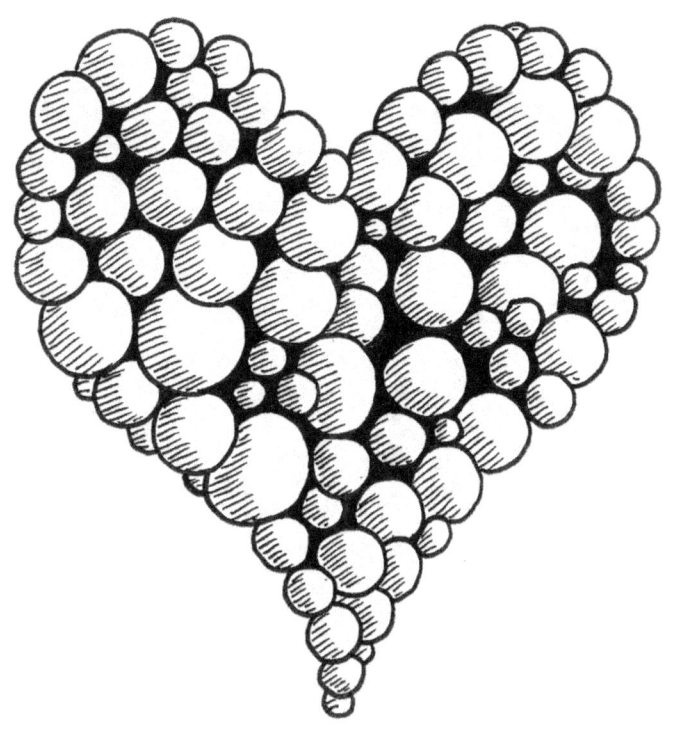

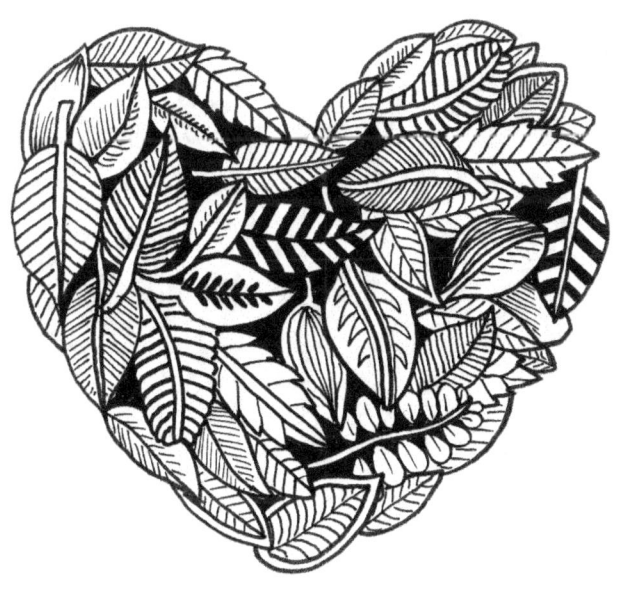

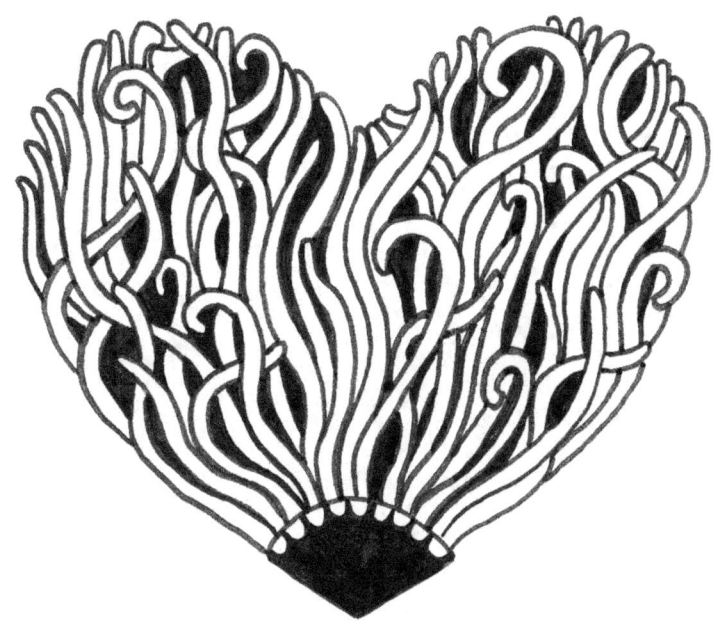
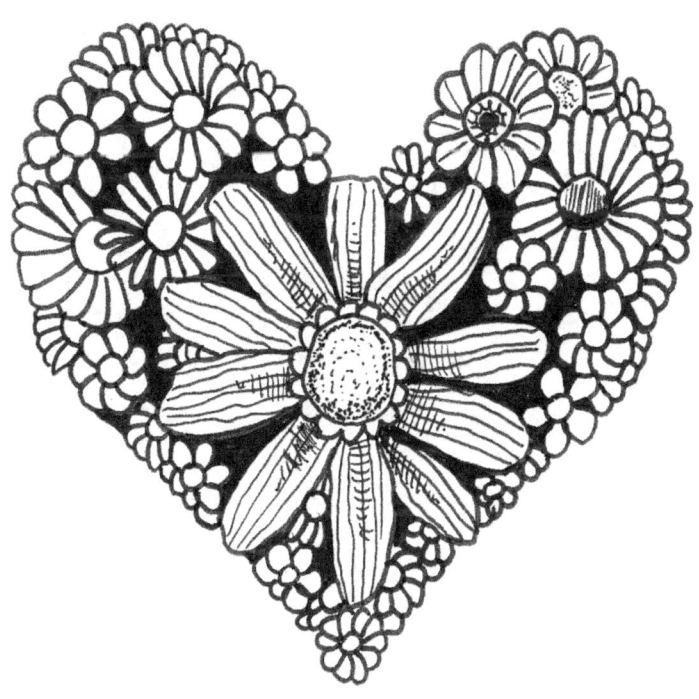

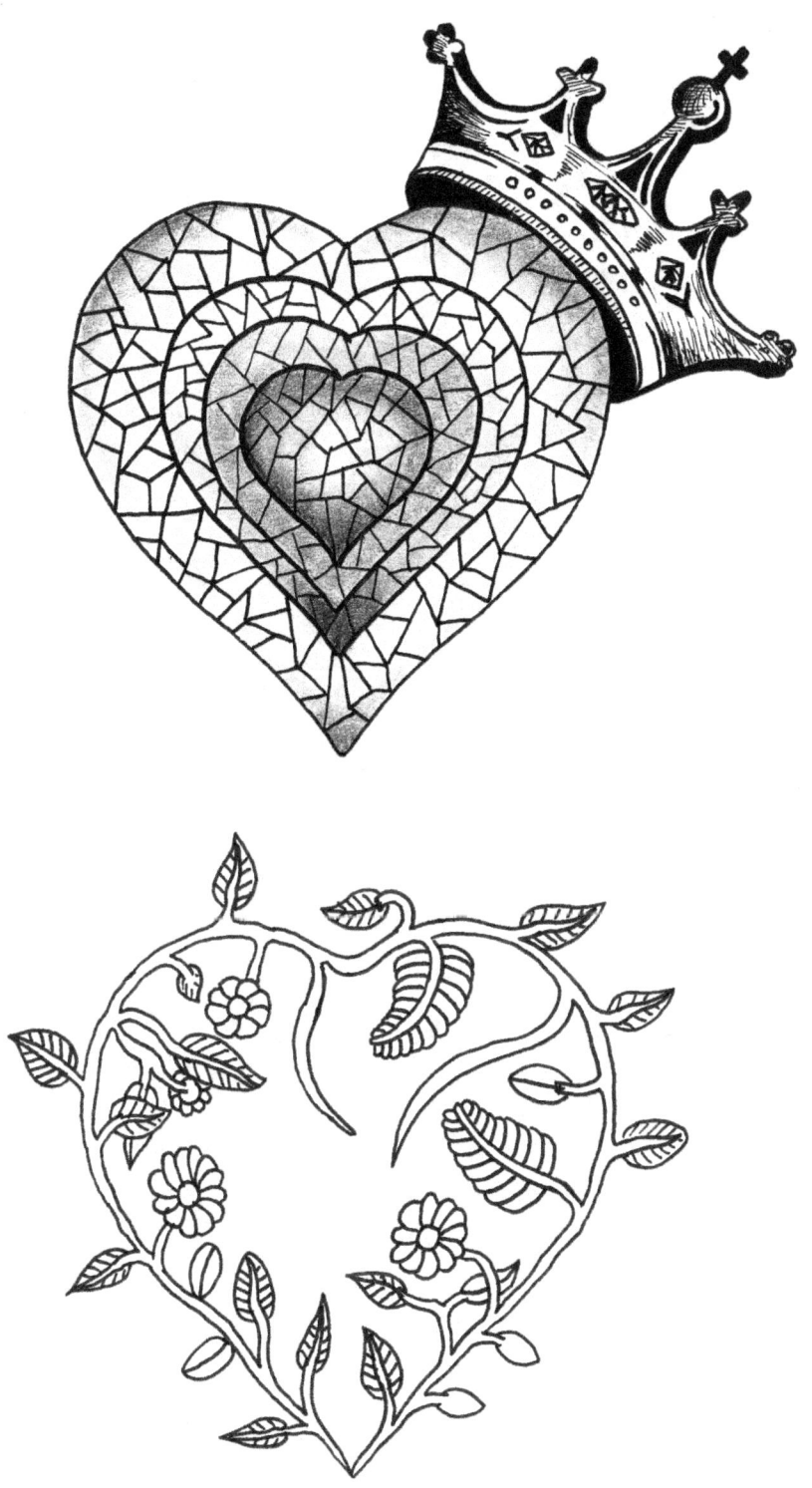

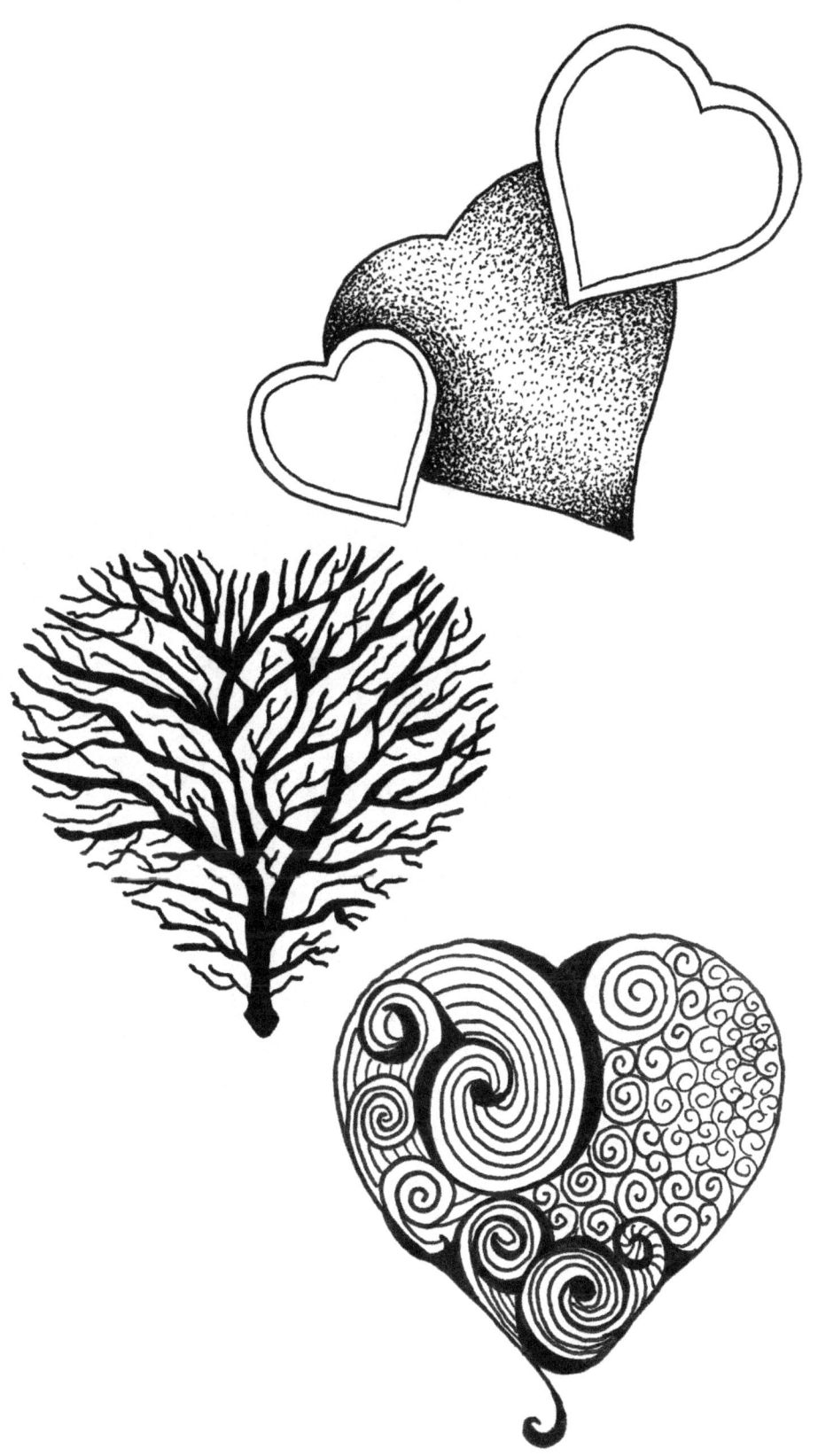

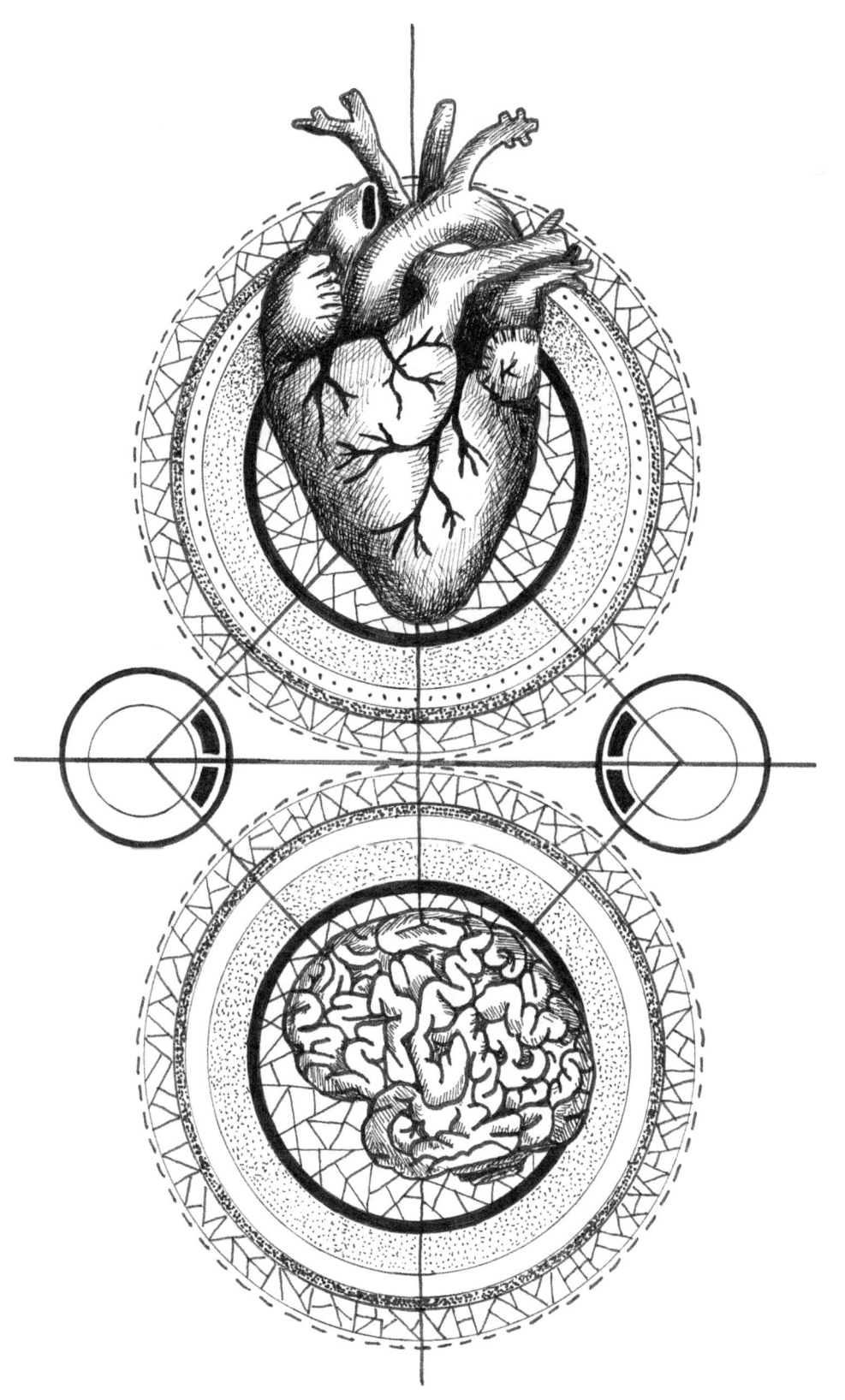

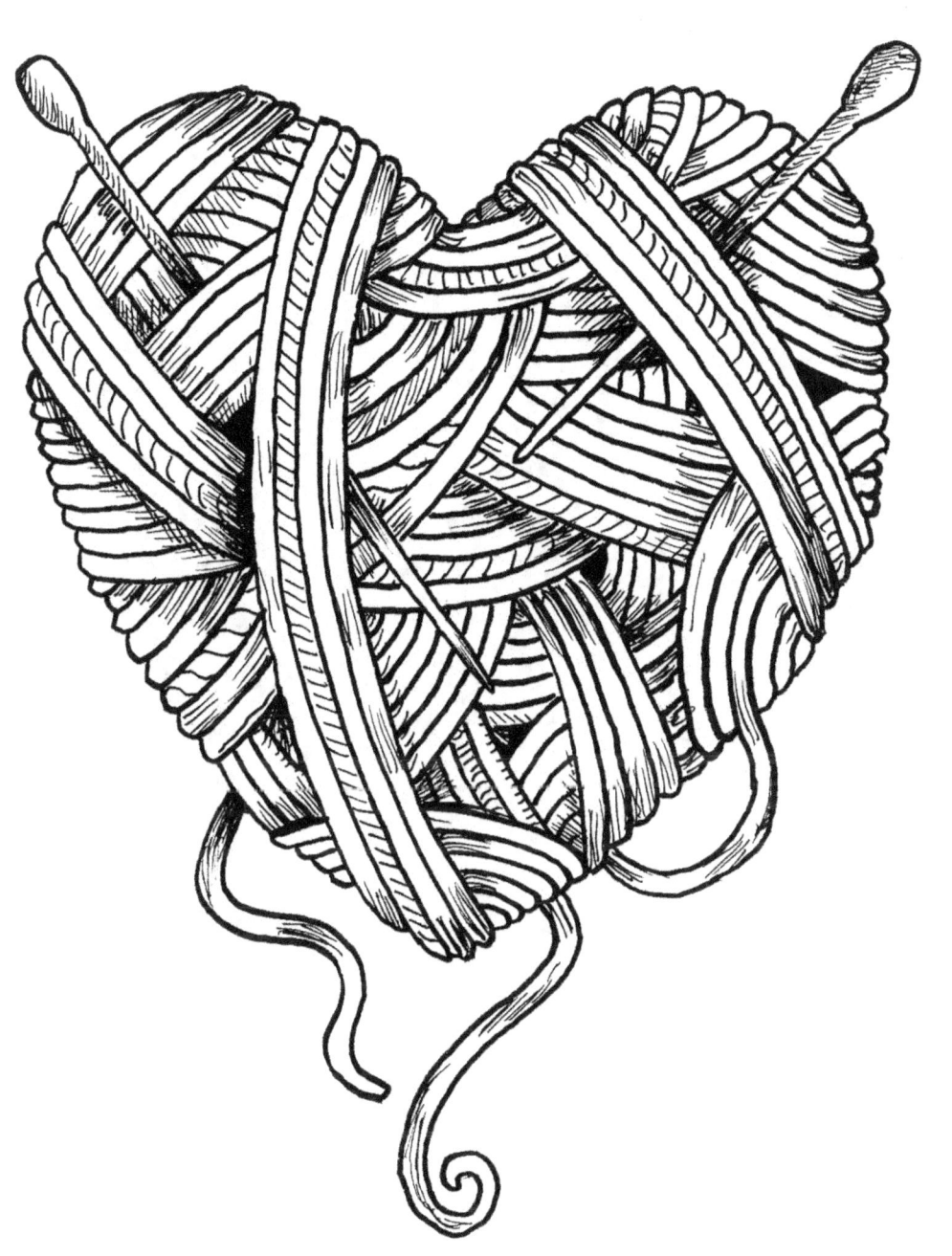

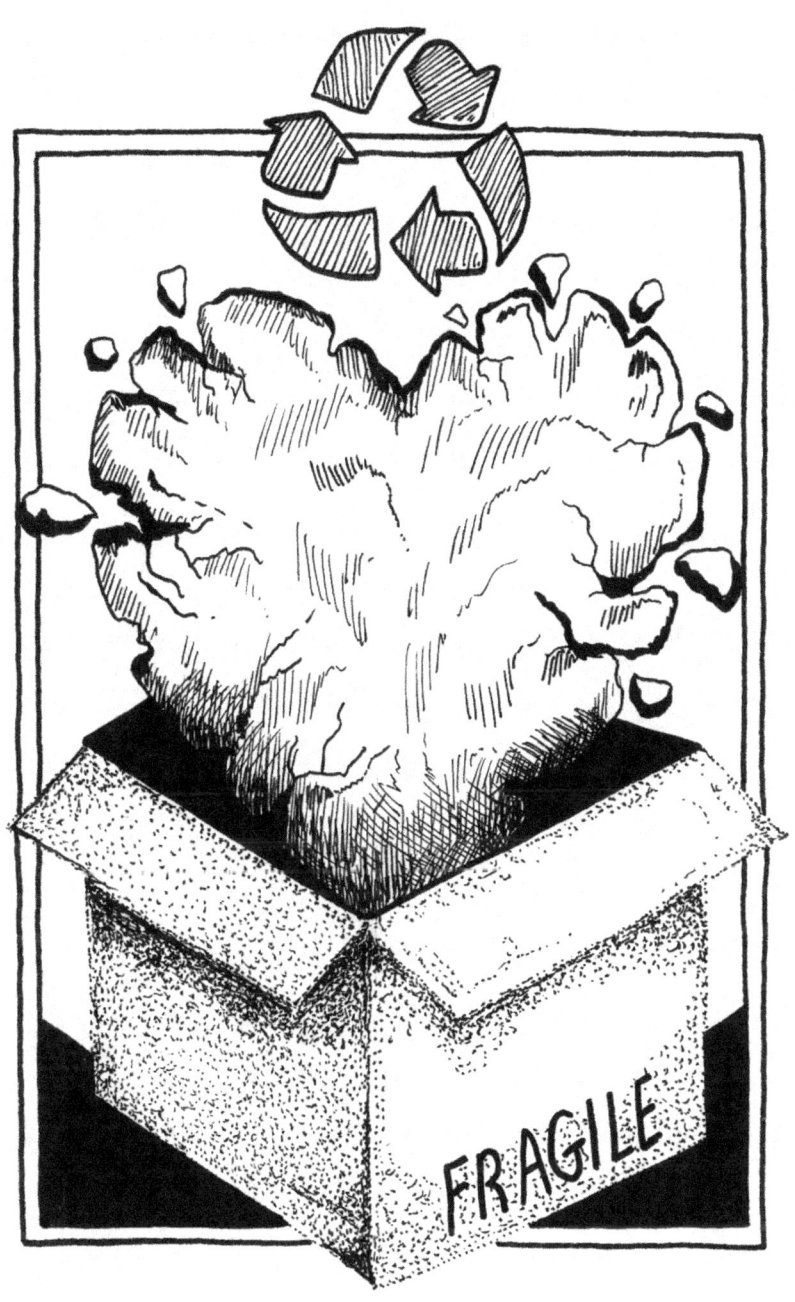

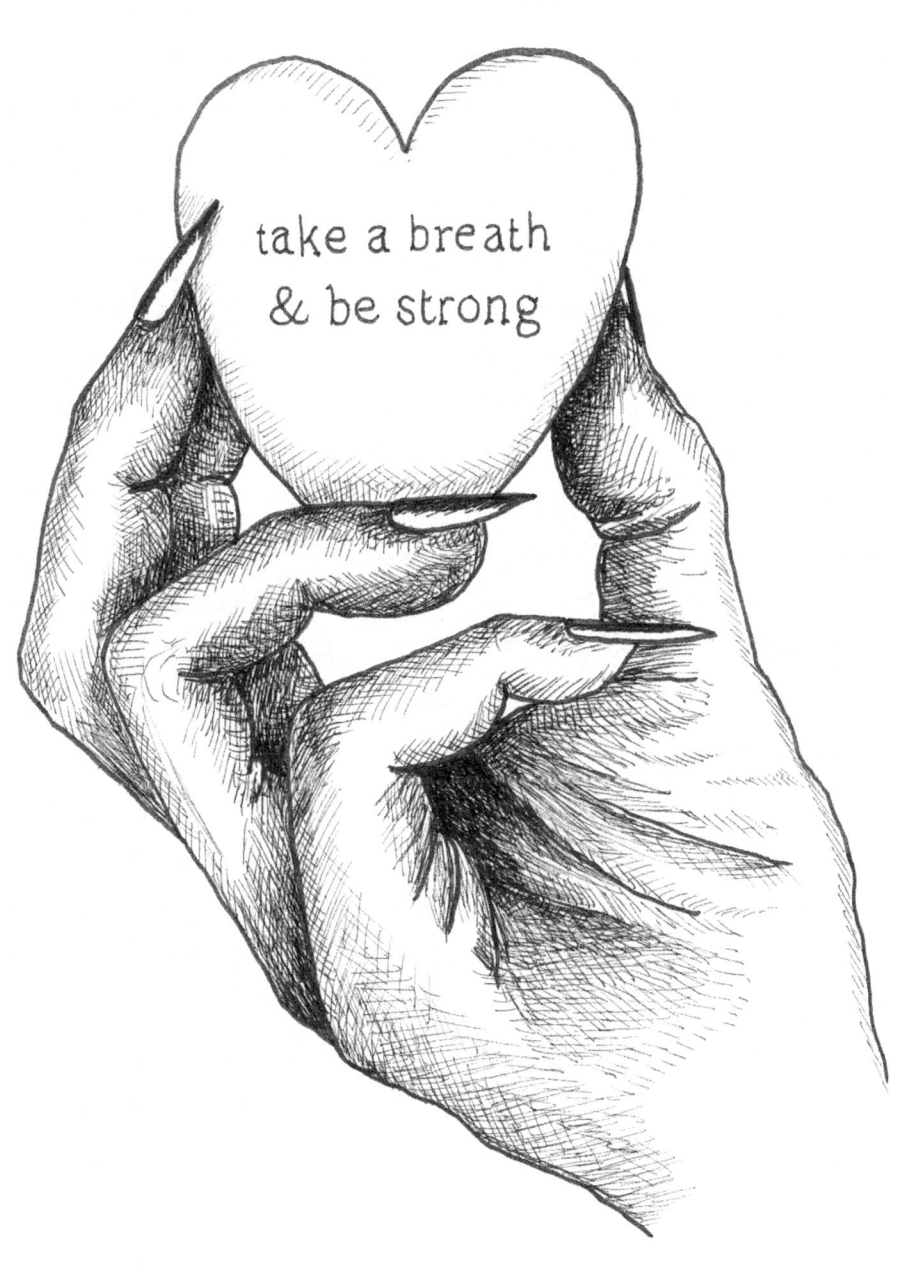

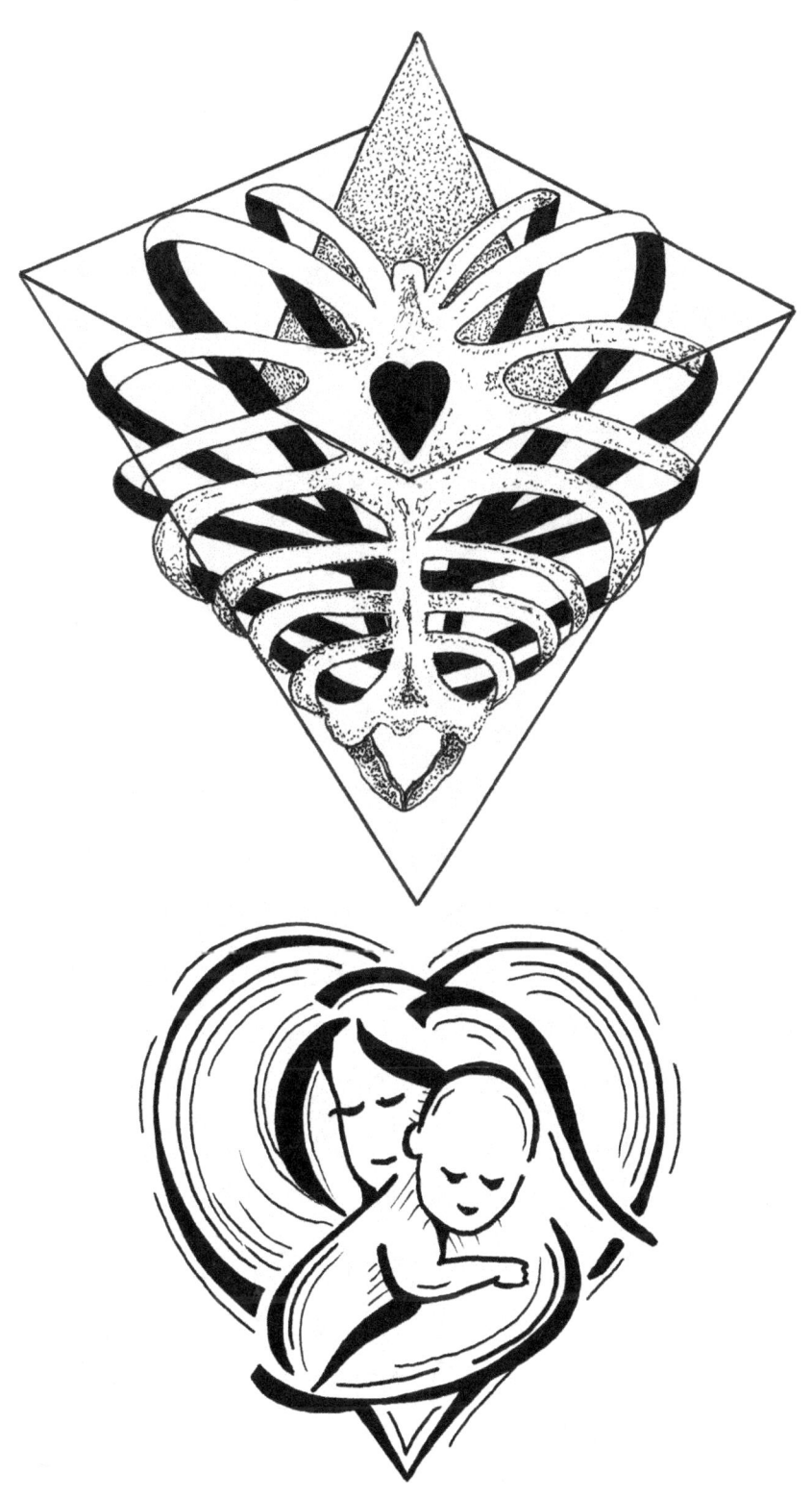

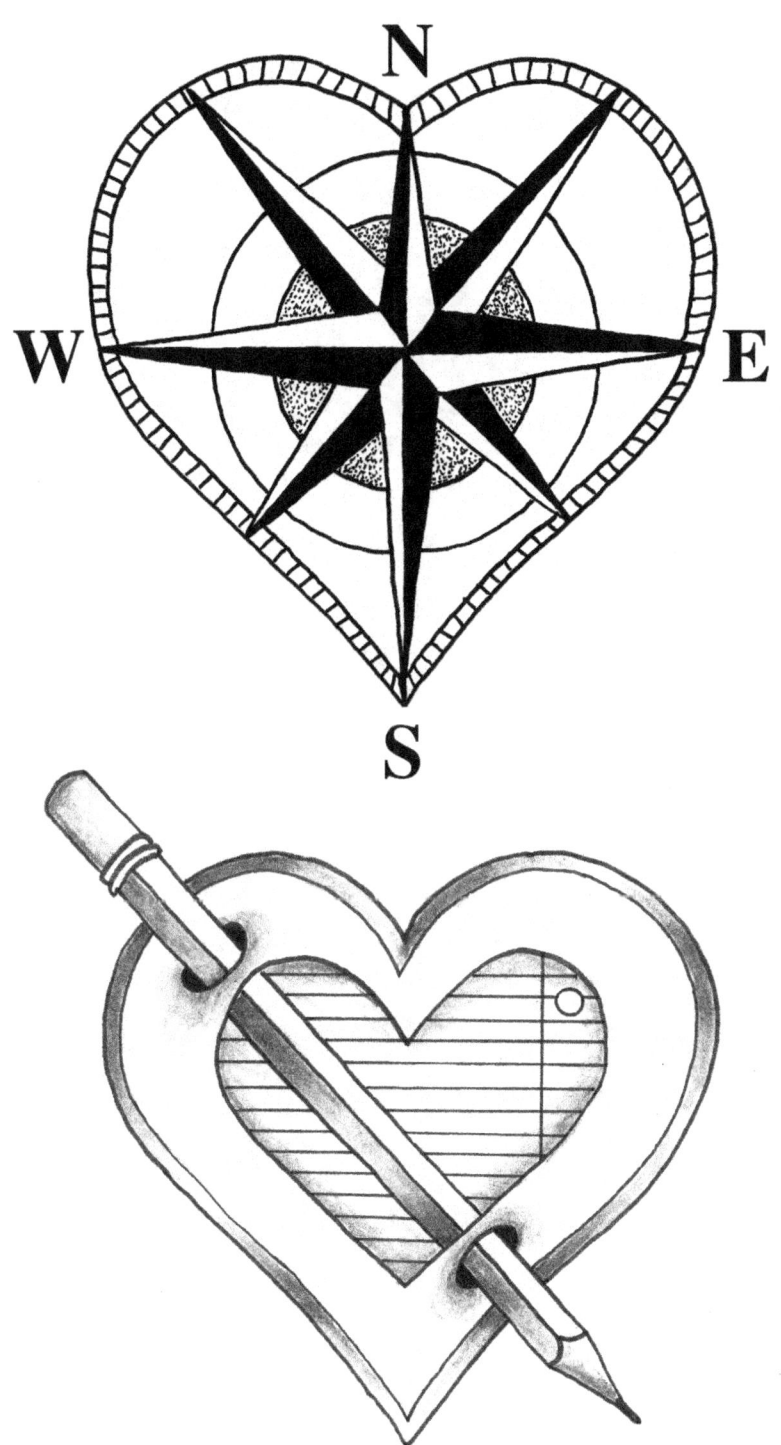

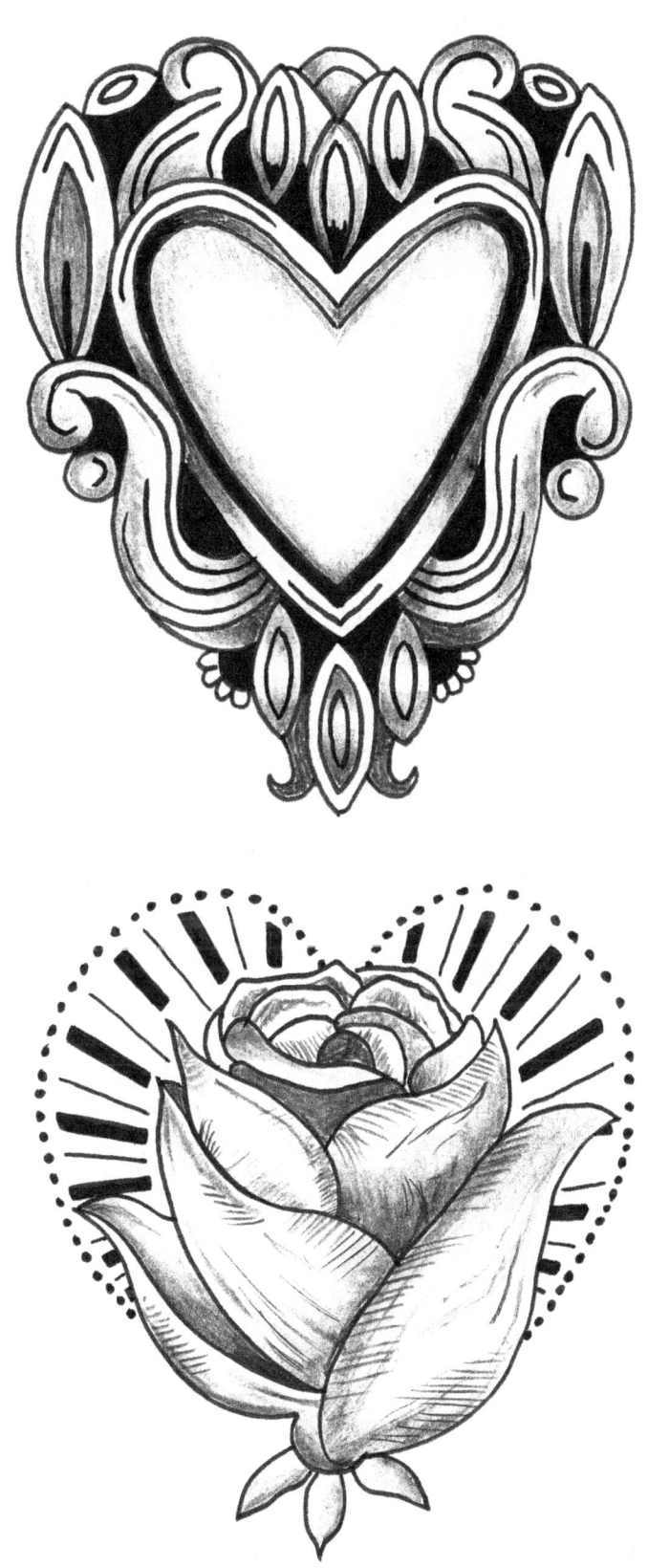

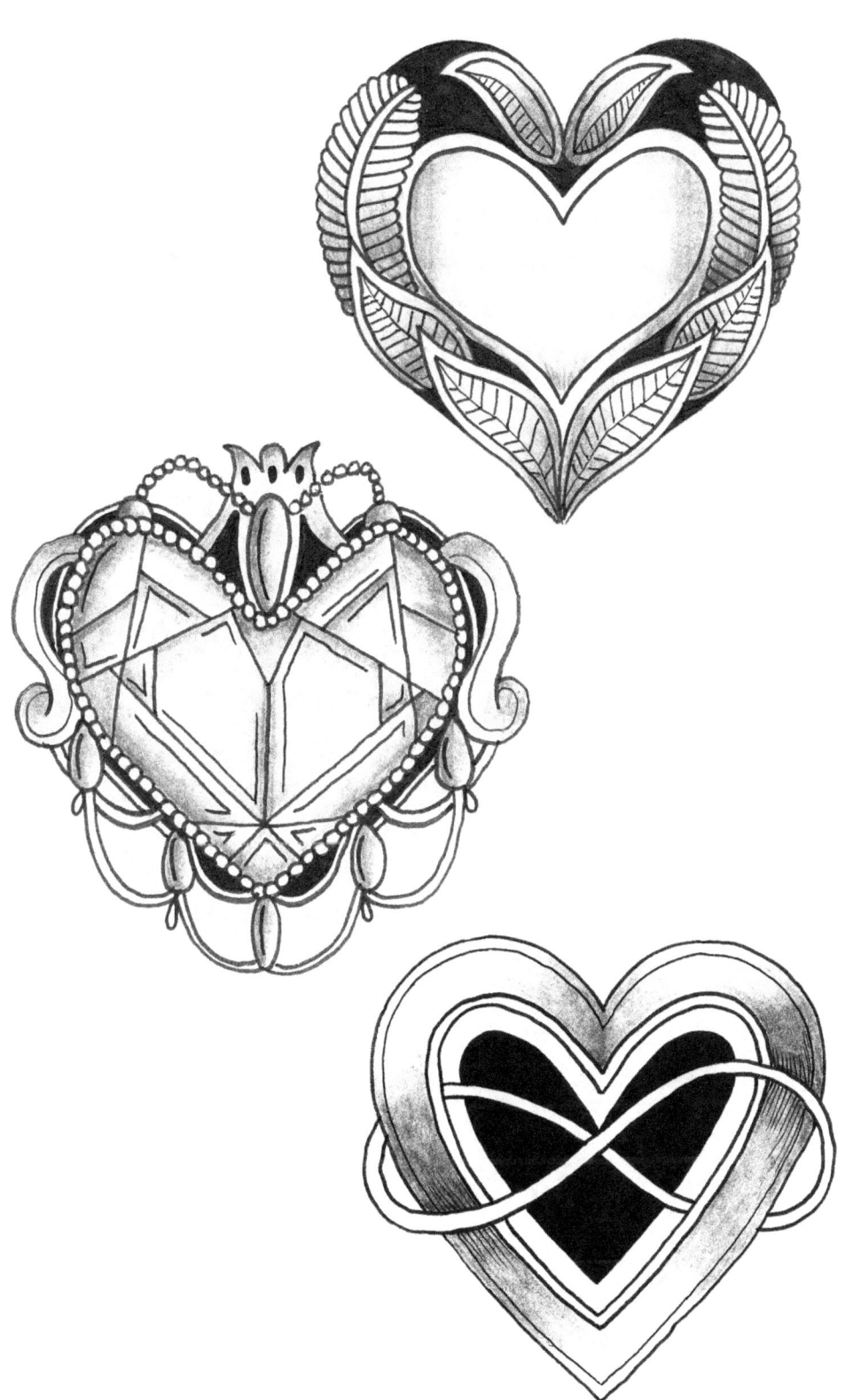

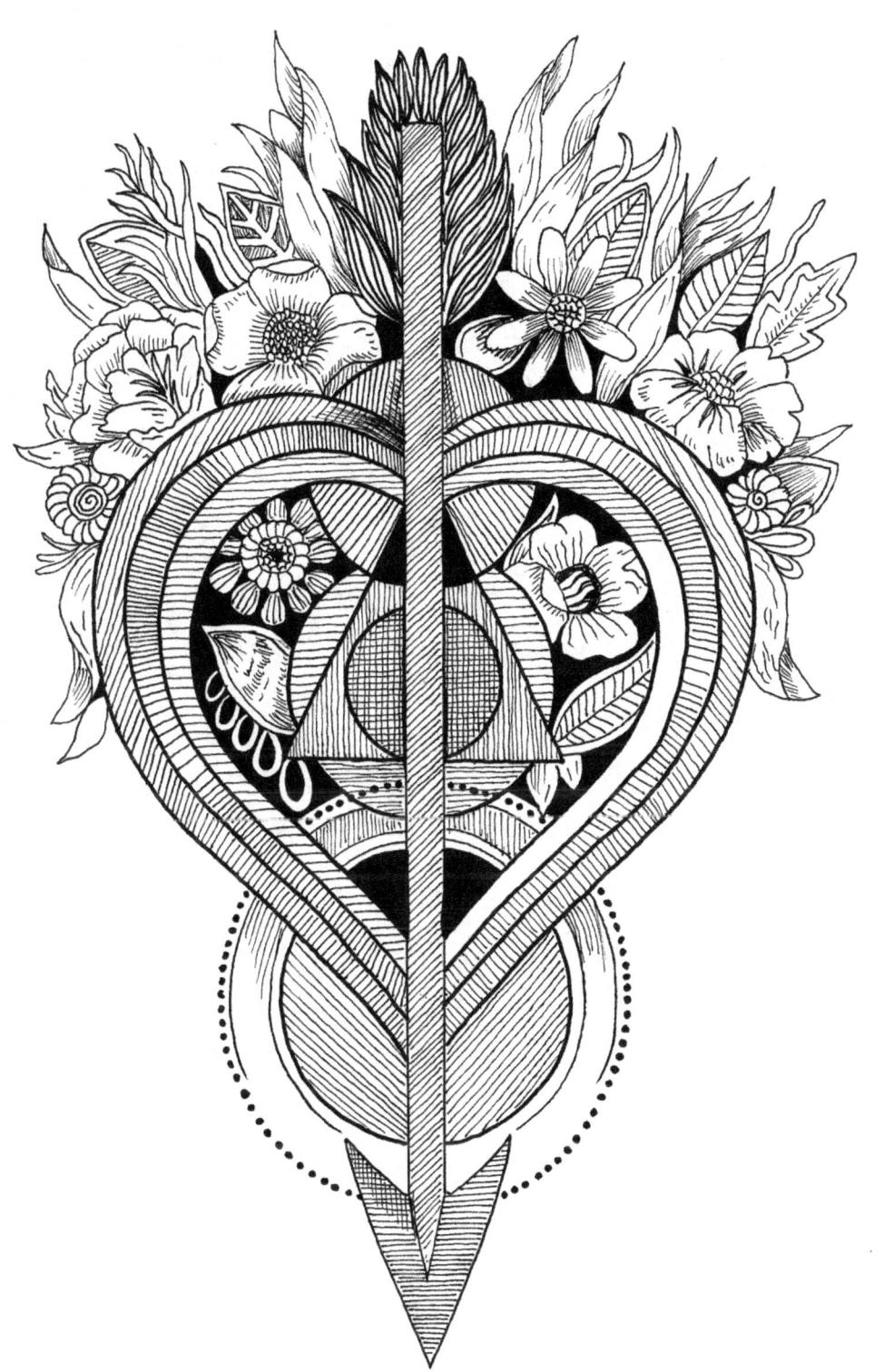

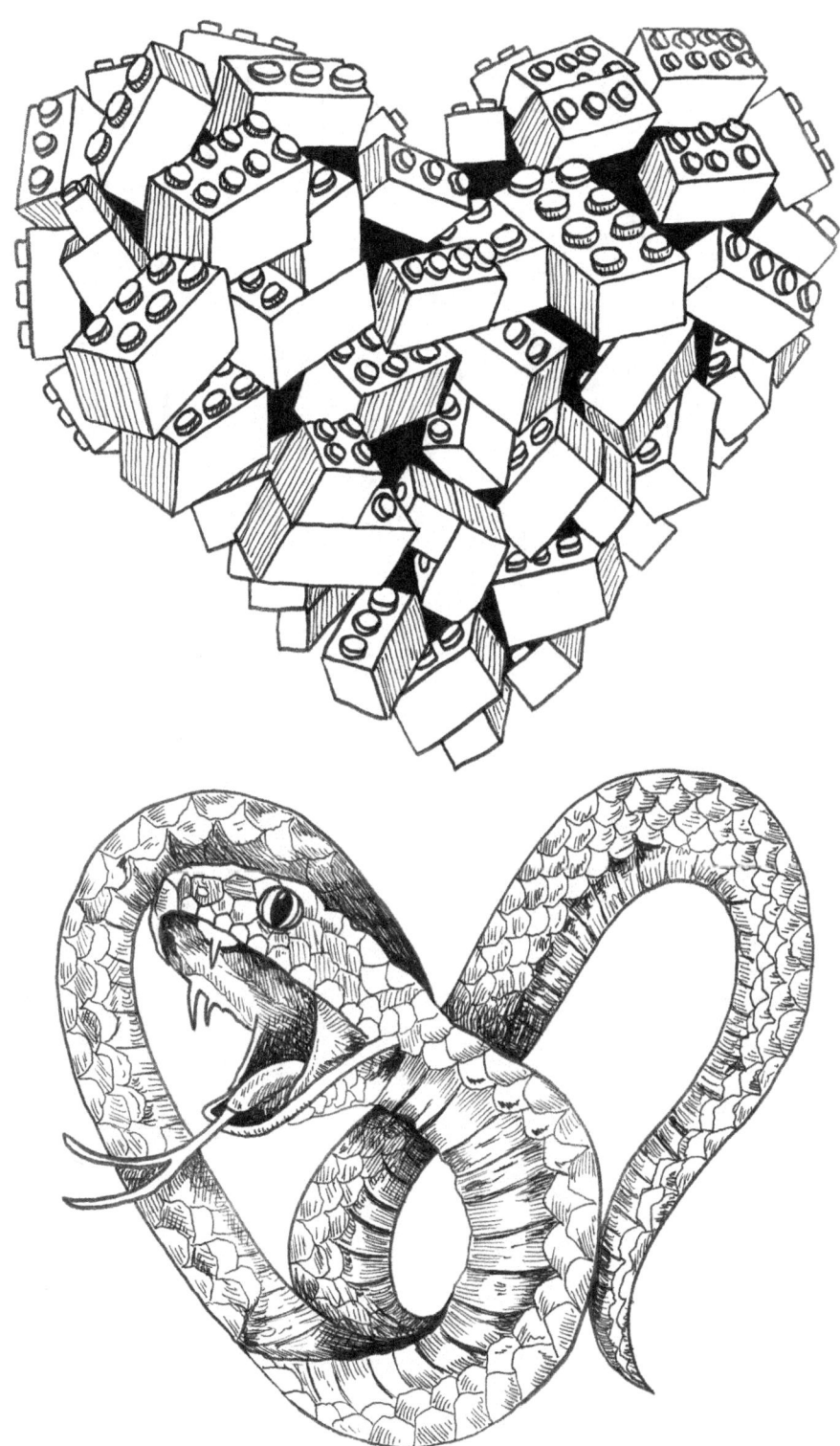

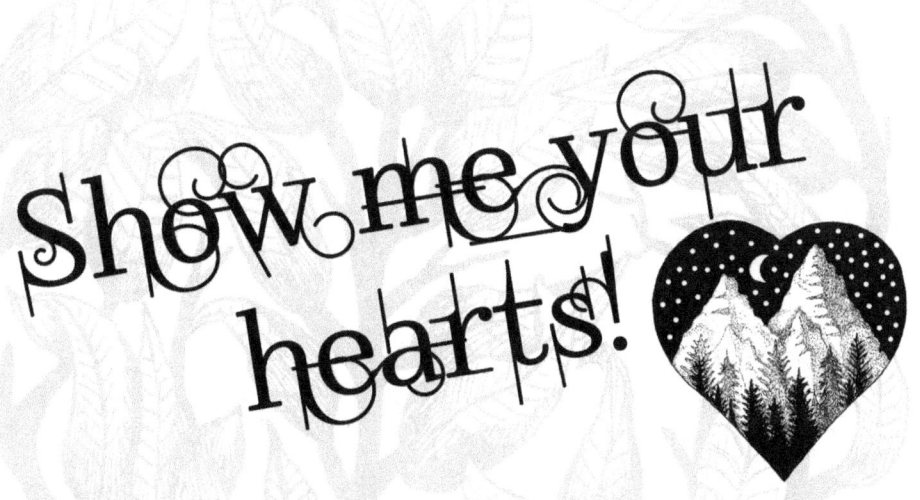

Show me your hearts!

I'd love to see what you do with the hearts in this book. Whether you color them, craft with them, make greetings cards, add them to projects, or even treat yourself to a heart tattoo for real!

 @squidoodleart

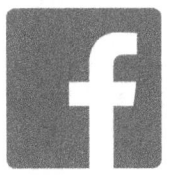 facebook.com/SquidDoodleArt

Make sure you follow me on instagram and facebook for regular giveaways and new book announcements!

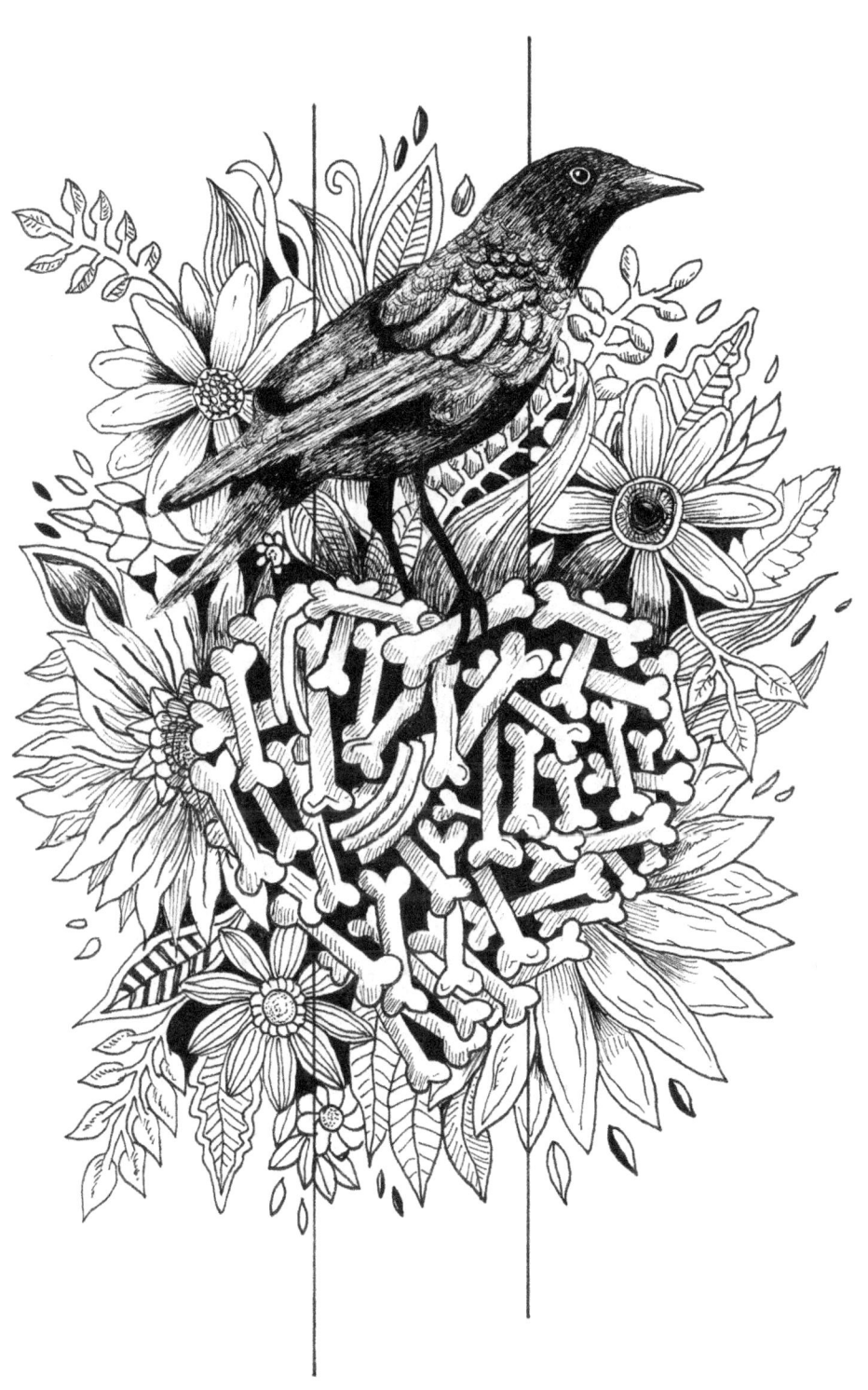

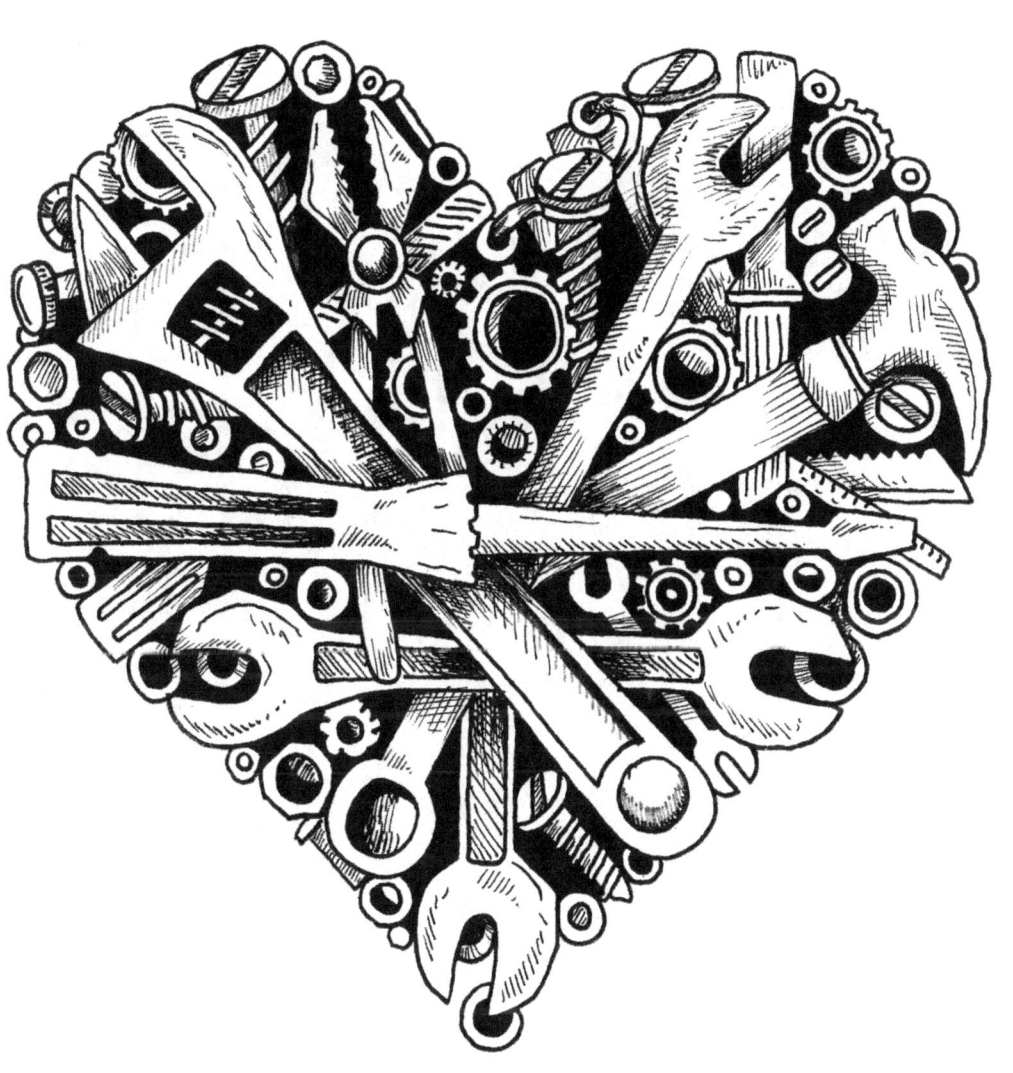

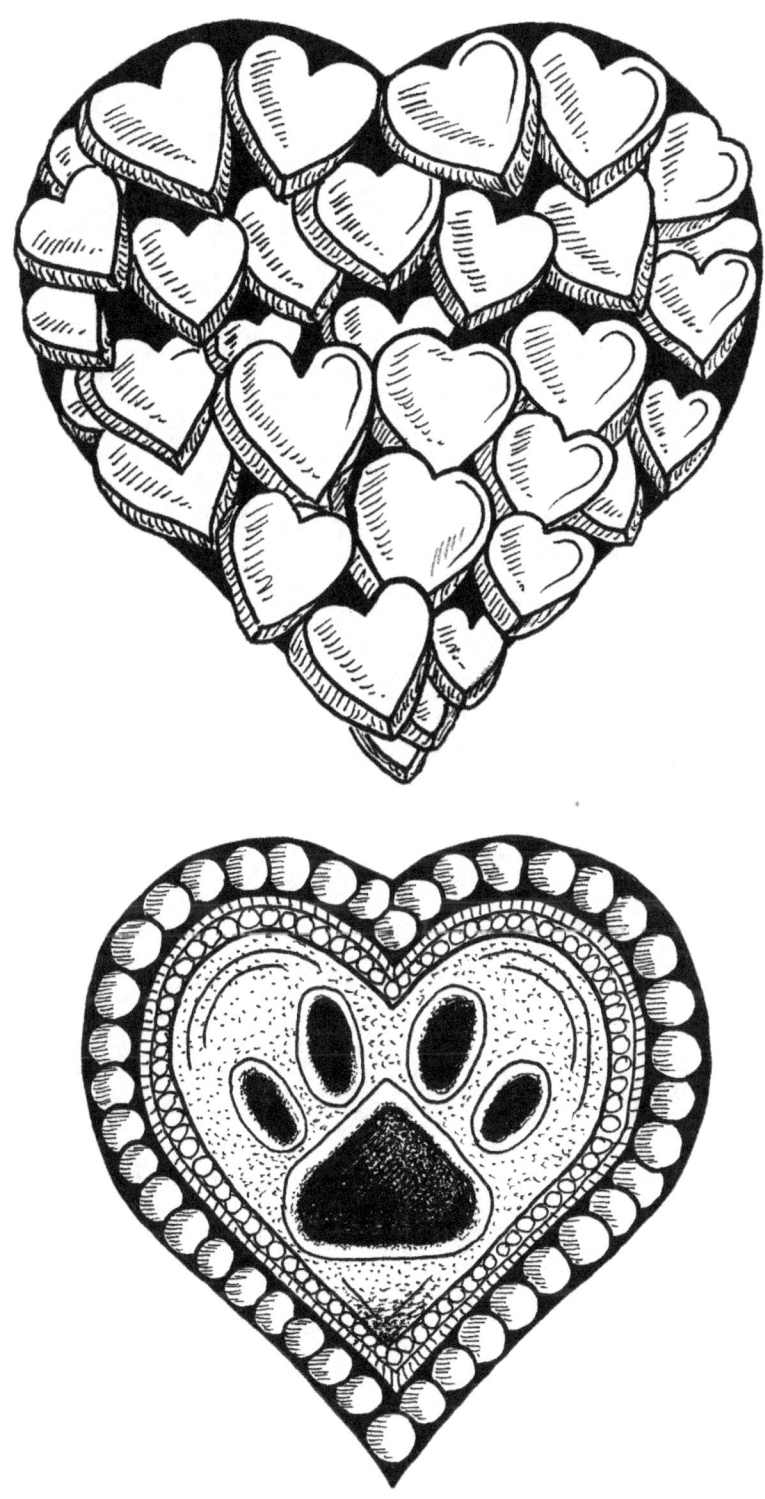

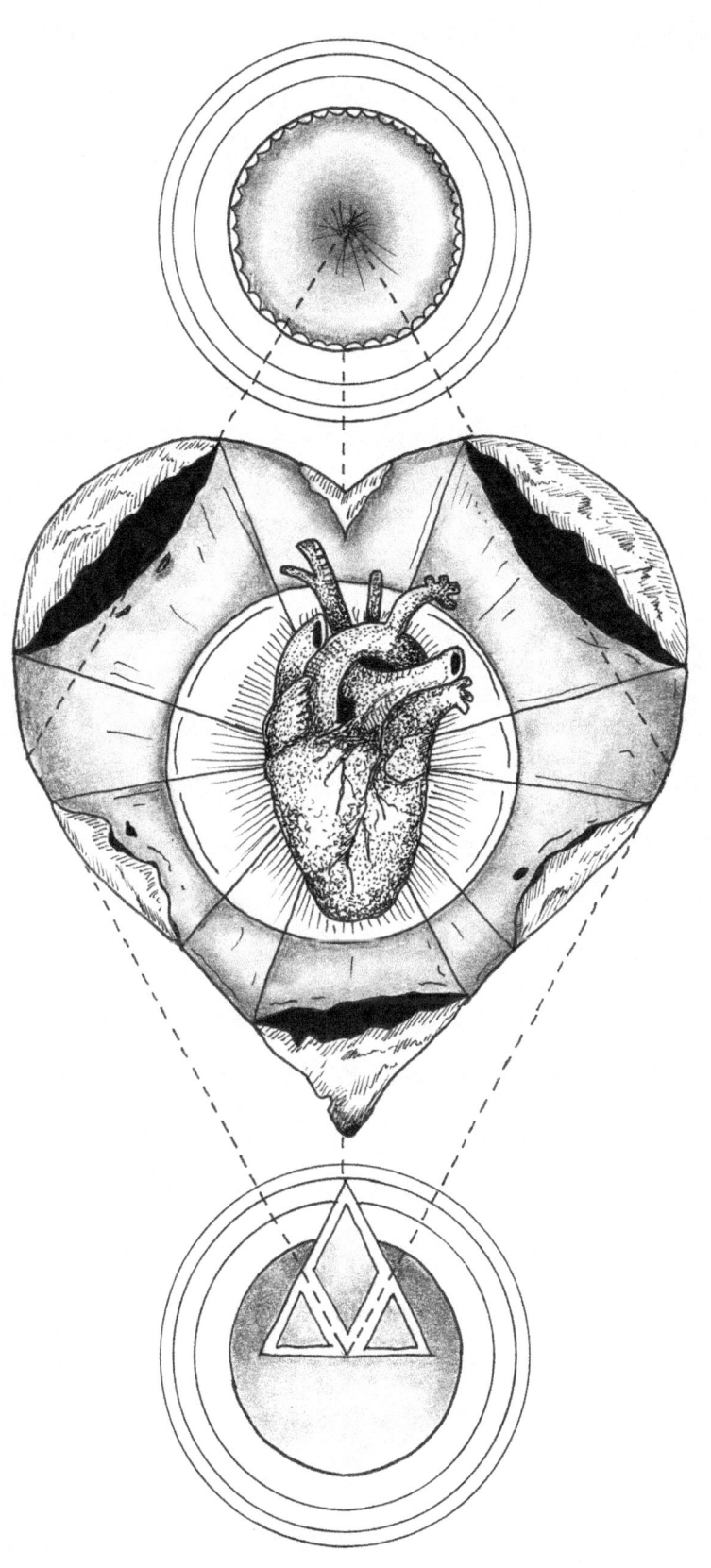

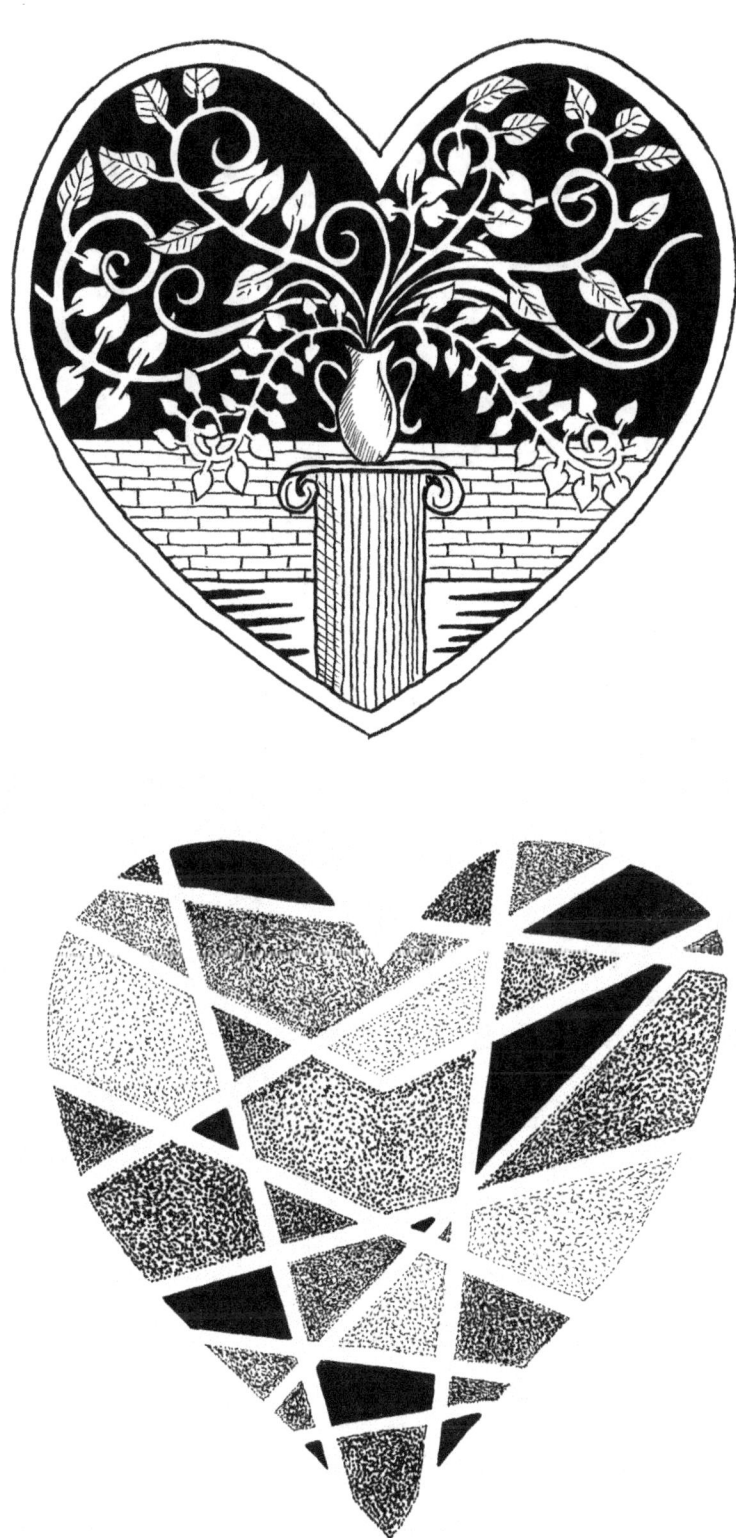

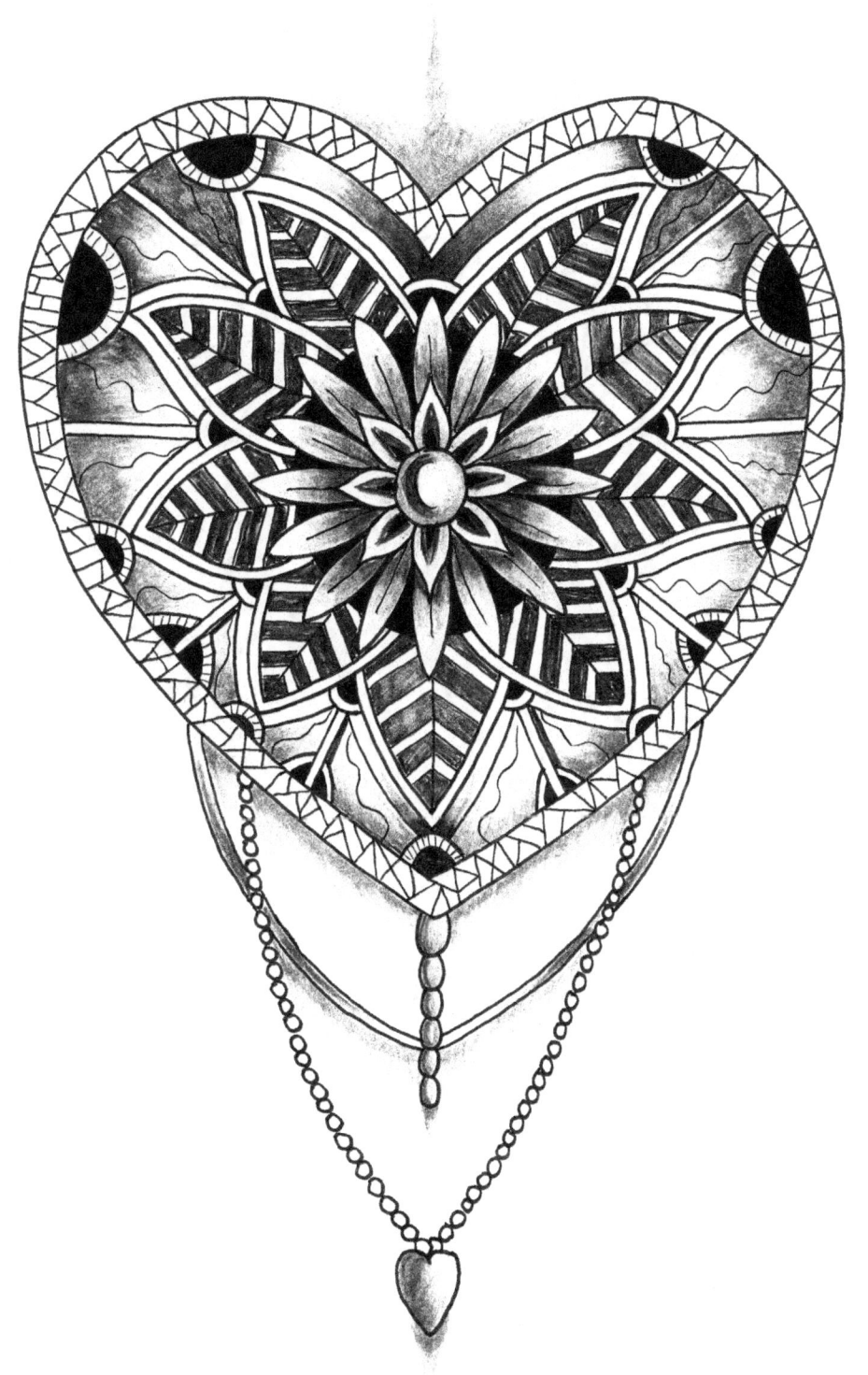

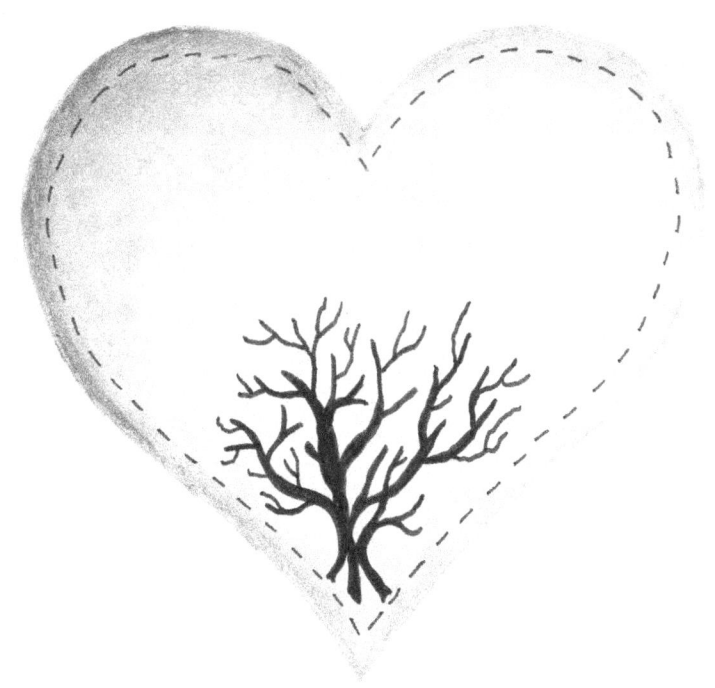

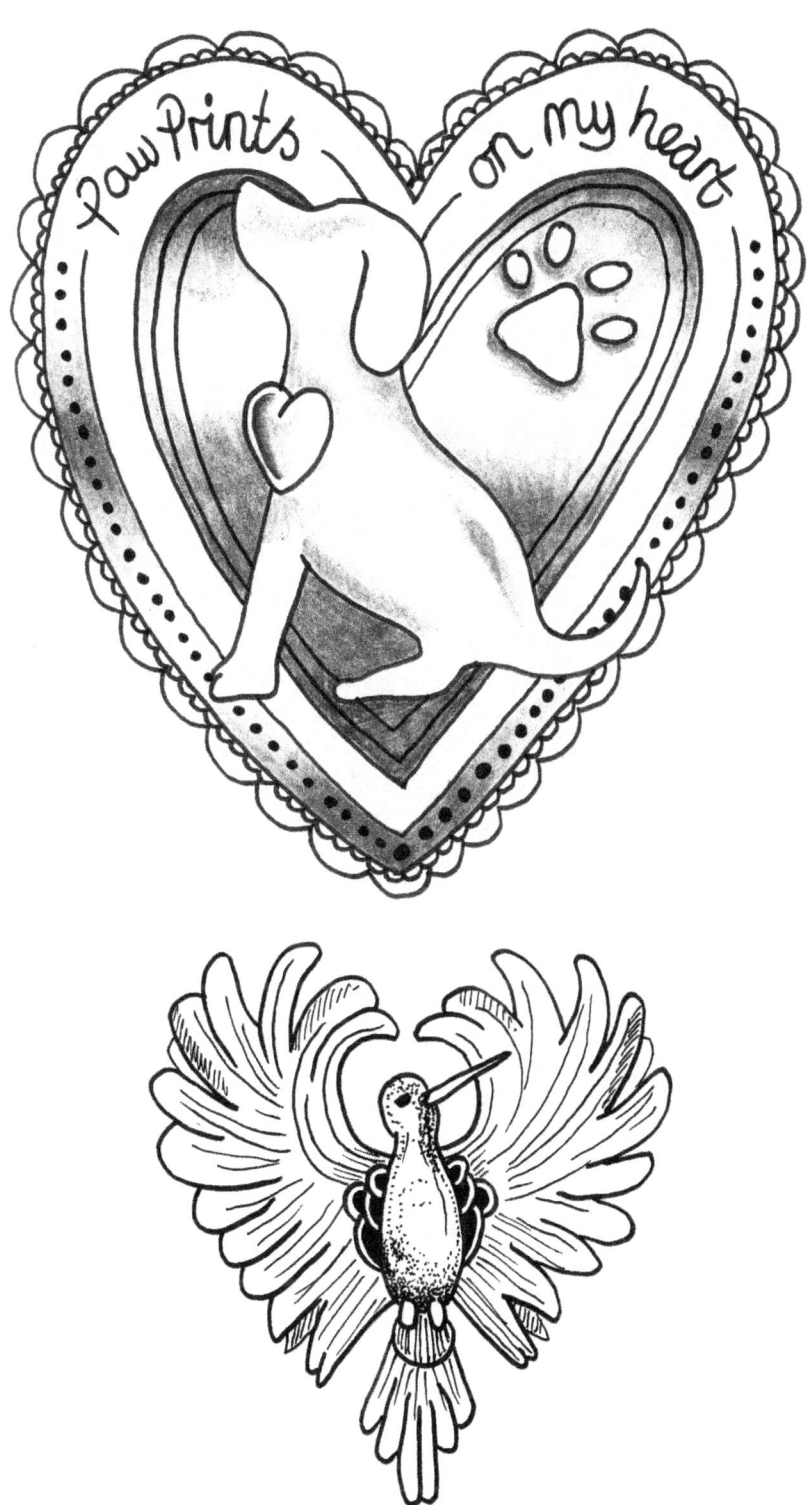

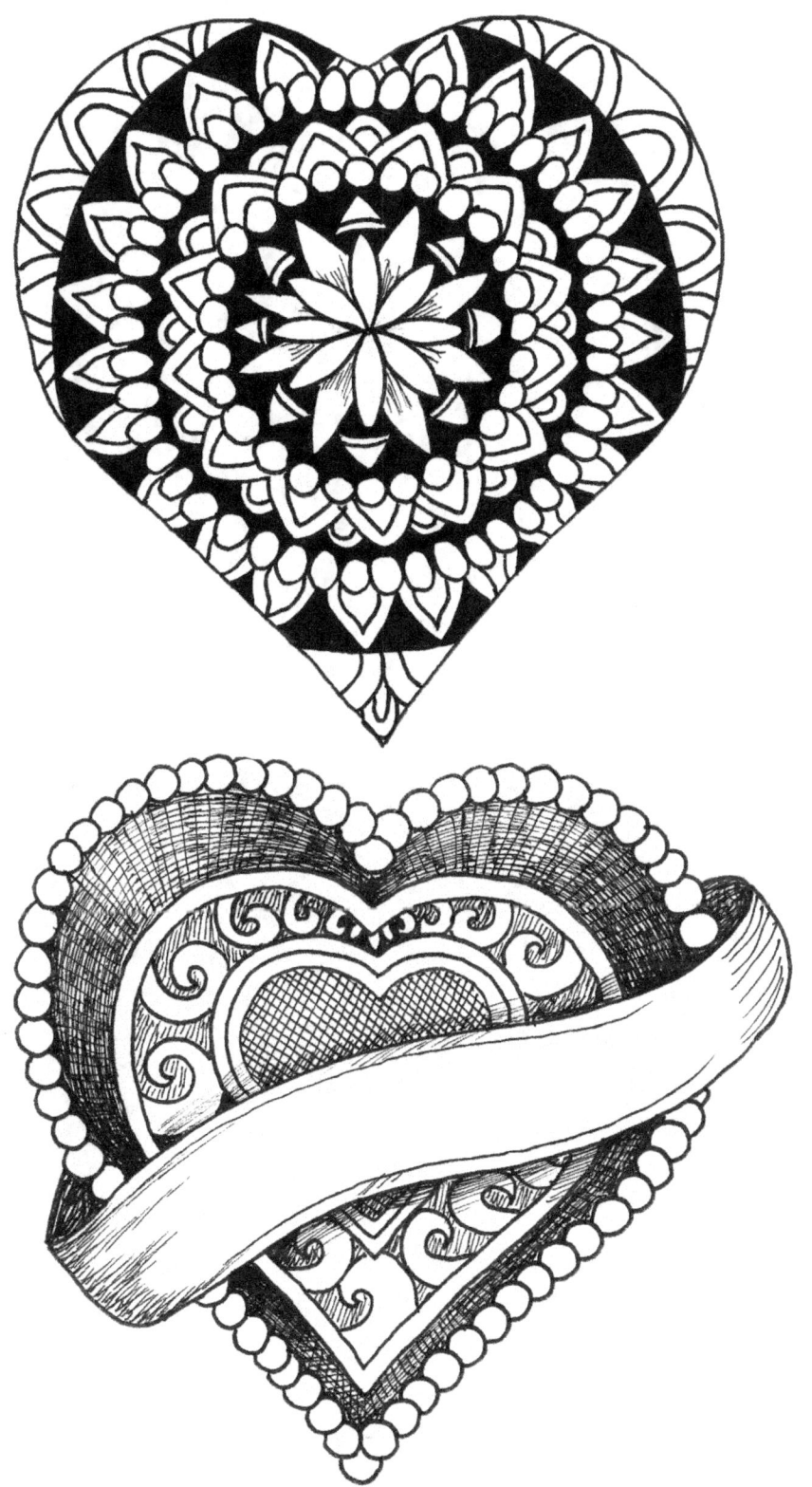

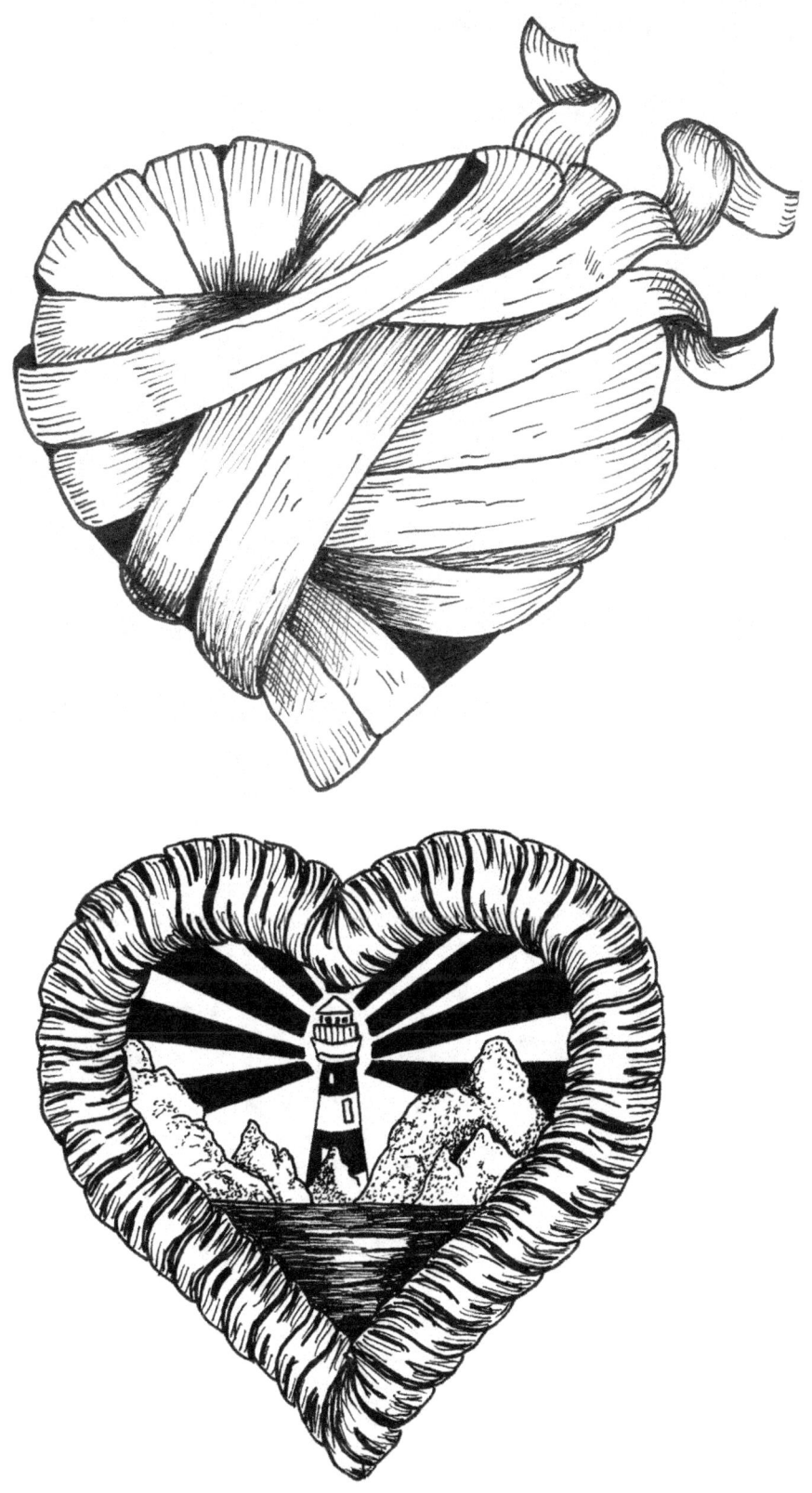

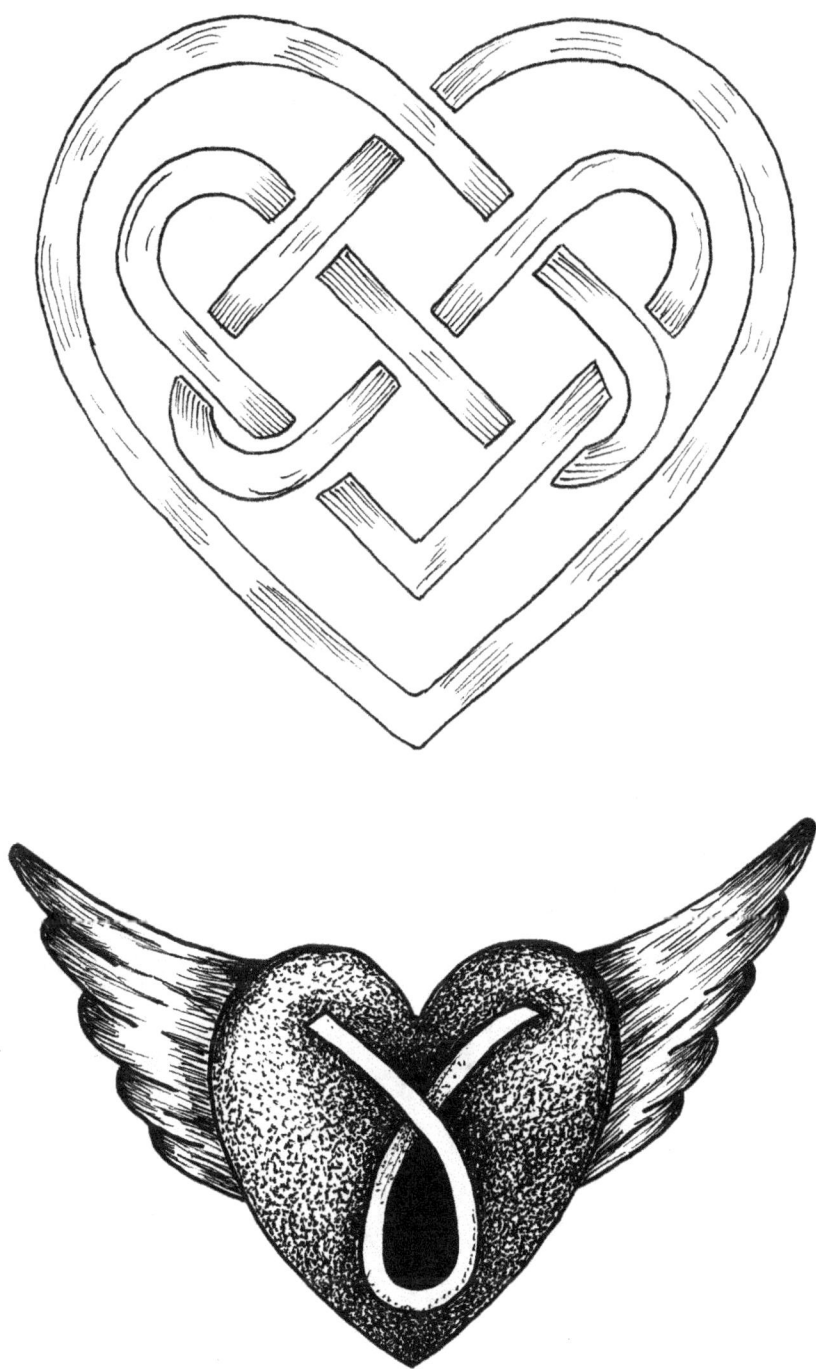

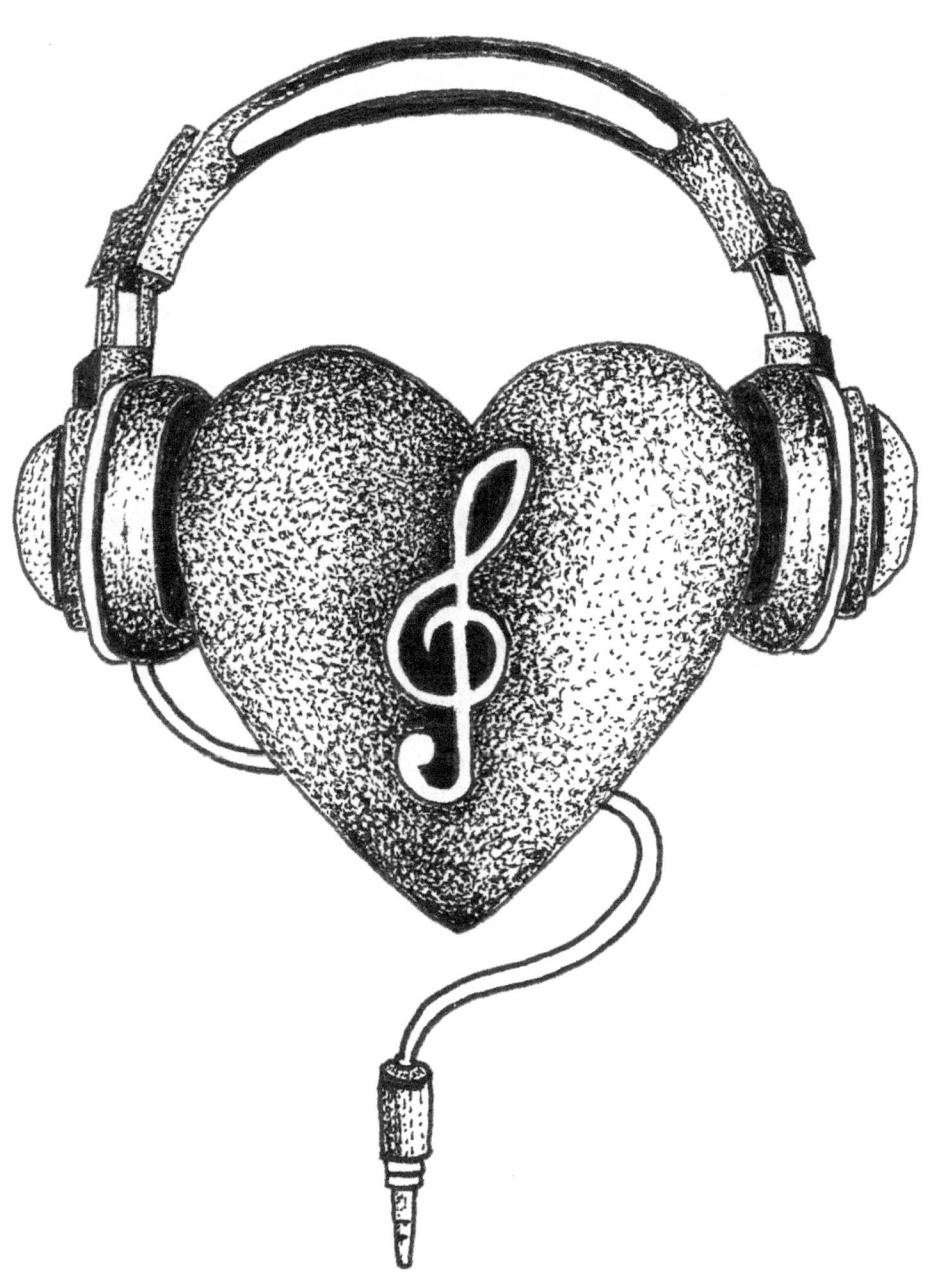

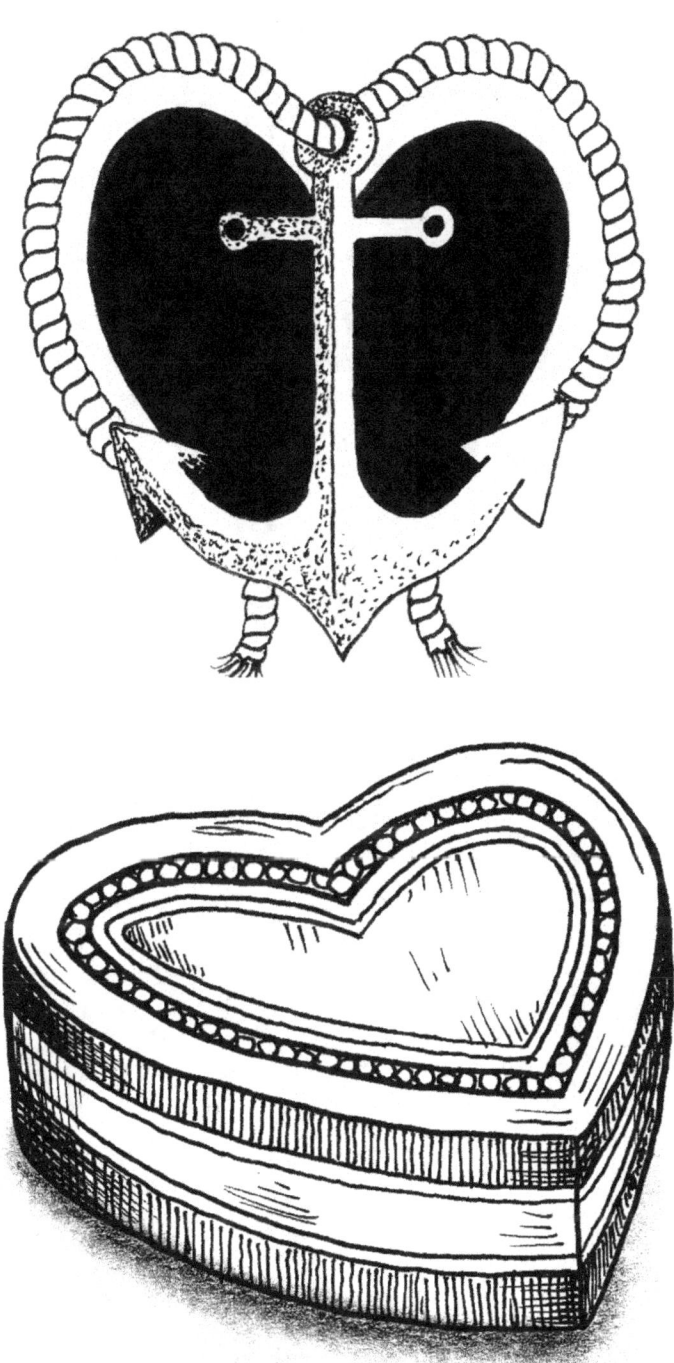

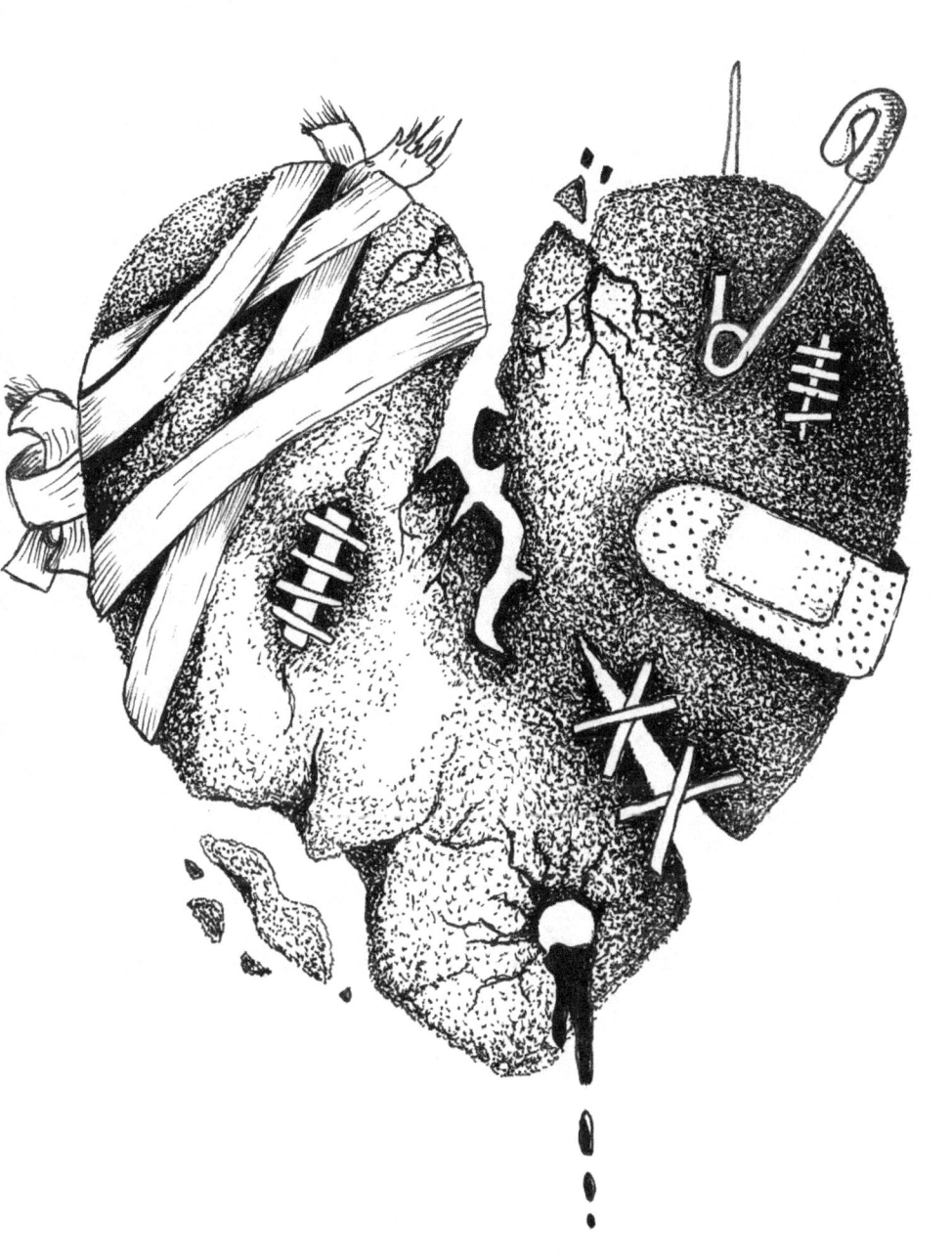

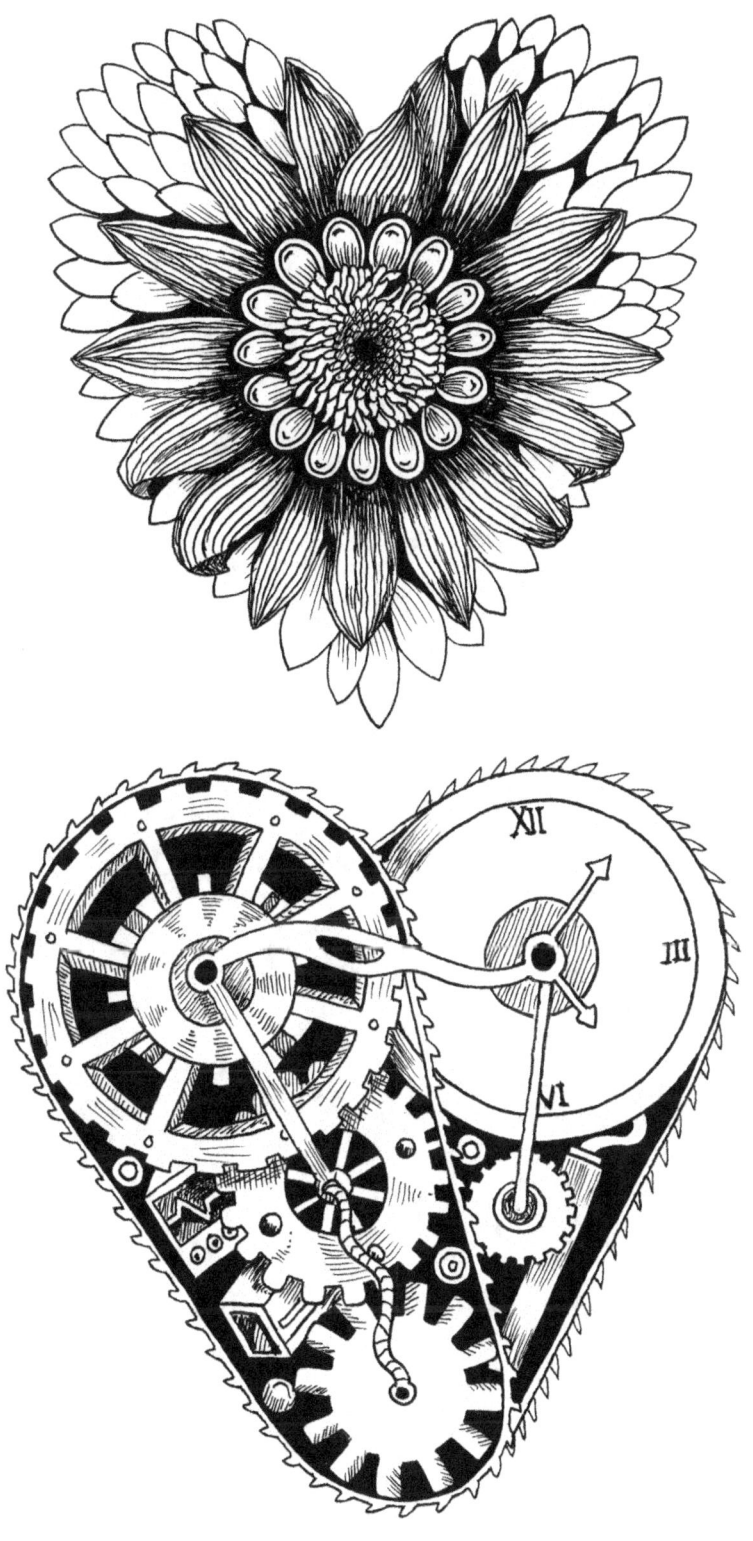

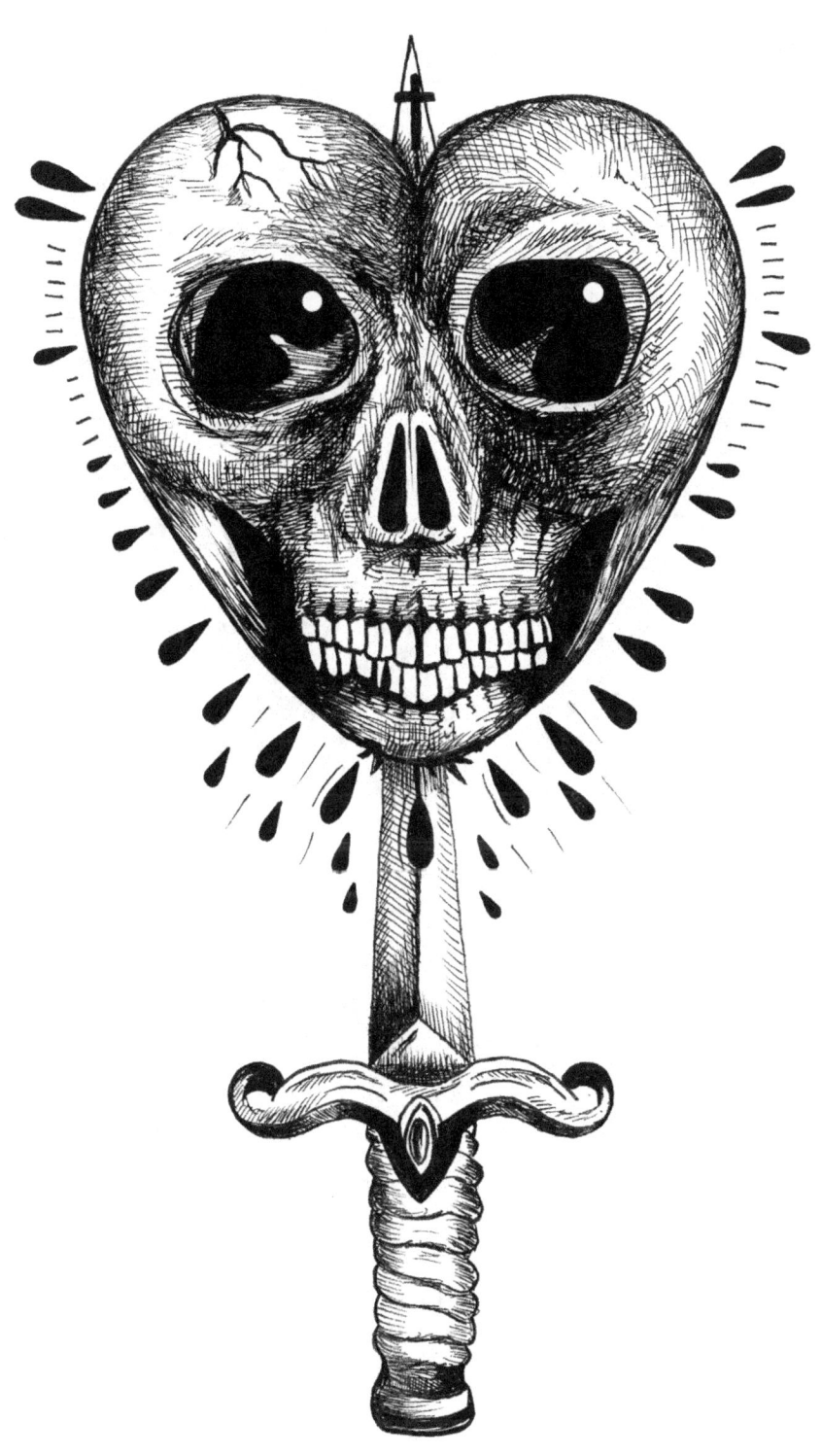

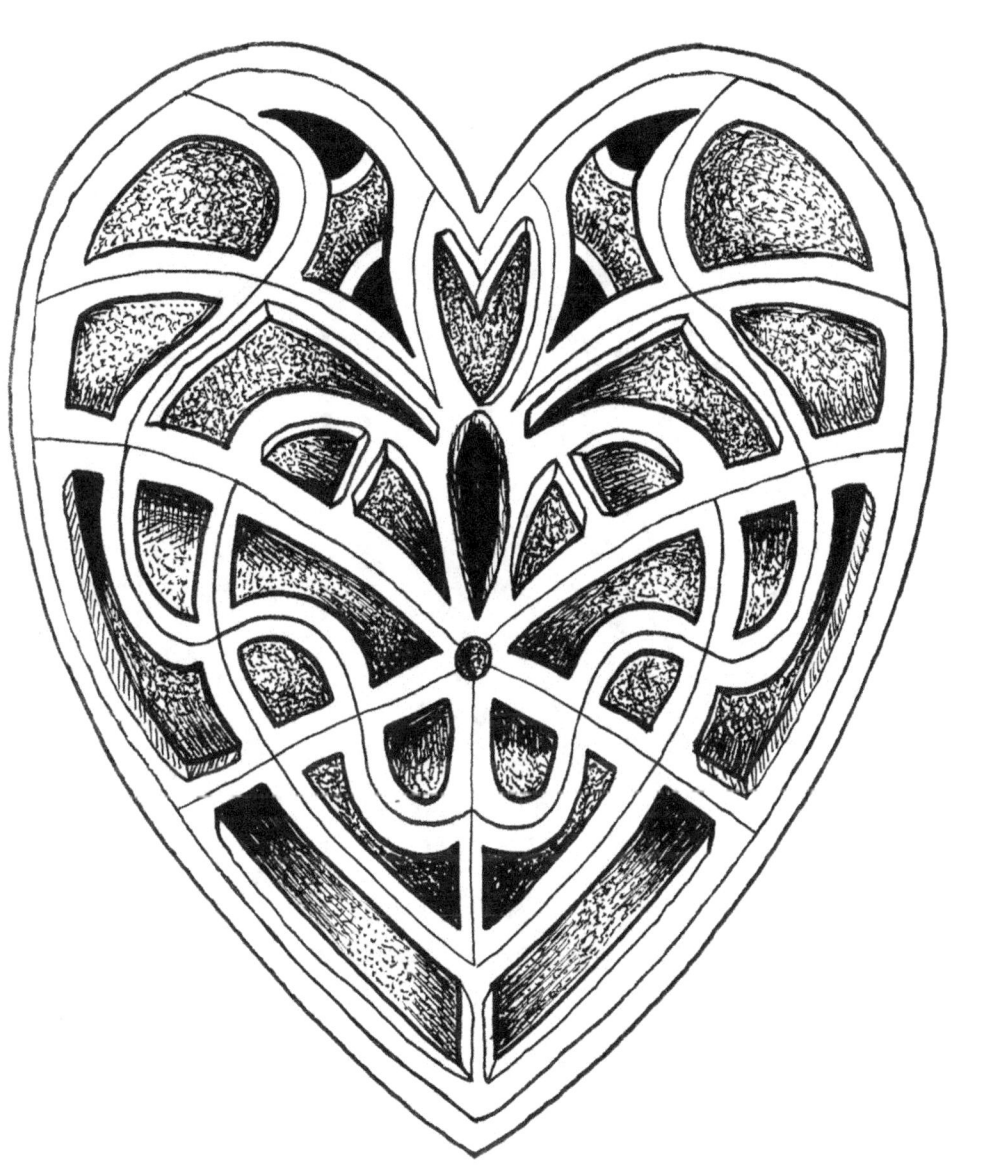

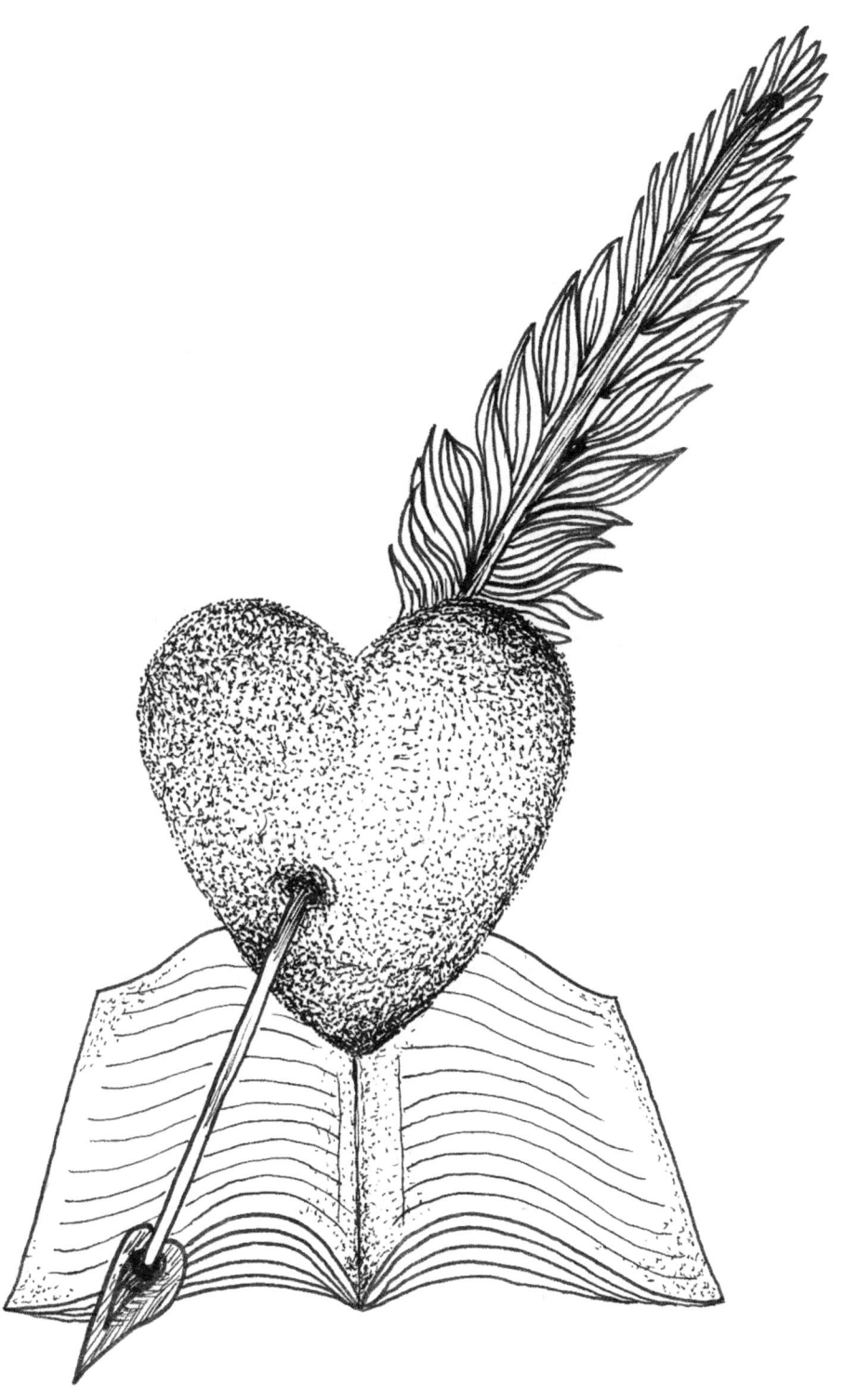

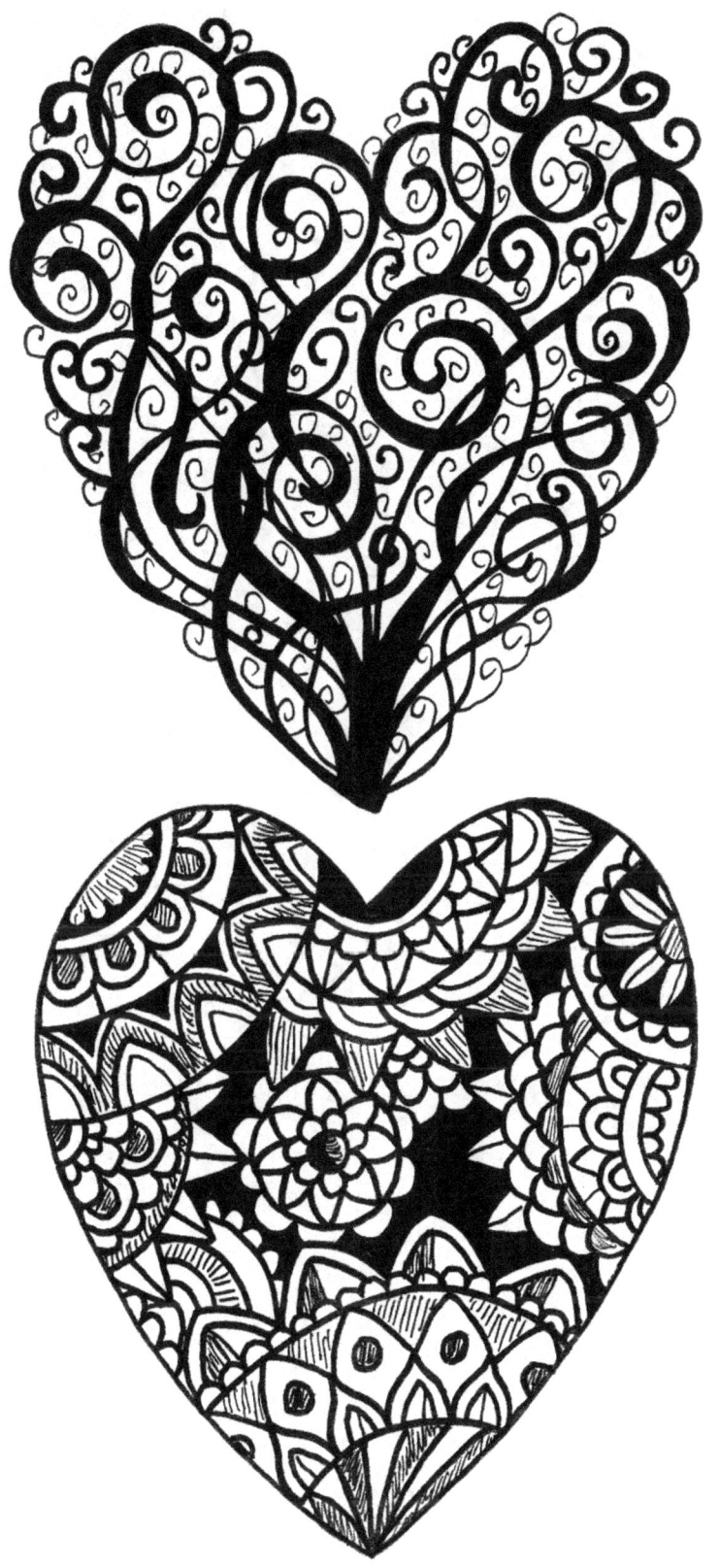

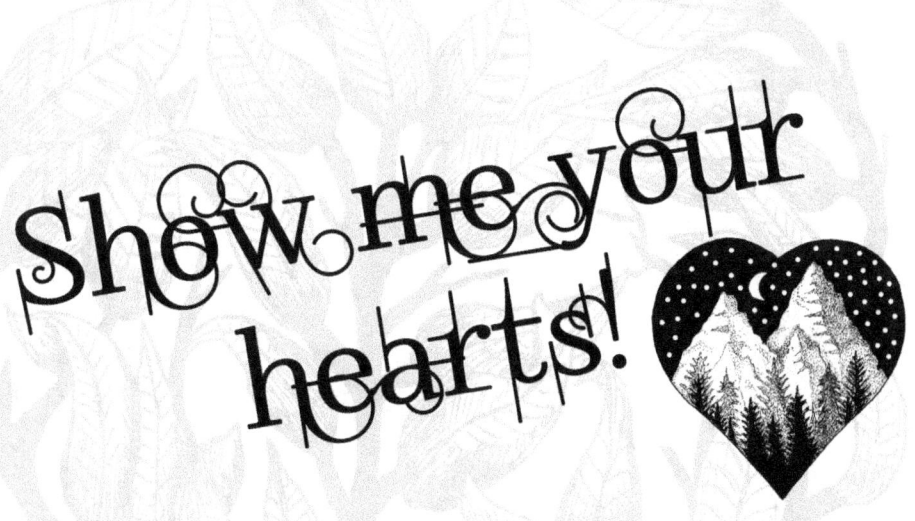

Show me your hearts!

I'd love to see what you do with the hearts in this book. Whether you color them, craft with them, make greetings cards, add them to projects, or even treat yourself to a heart tattoo for real!

 @squidoodleart

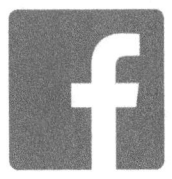 facebook.com/SquidDoodleArt

Make sure you follow me on instagram and facebook for regular giveaways and new book announcements!

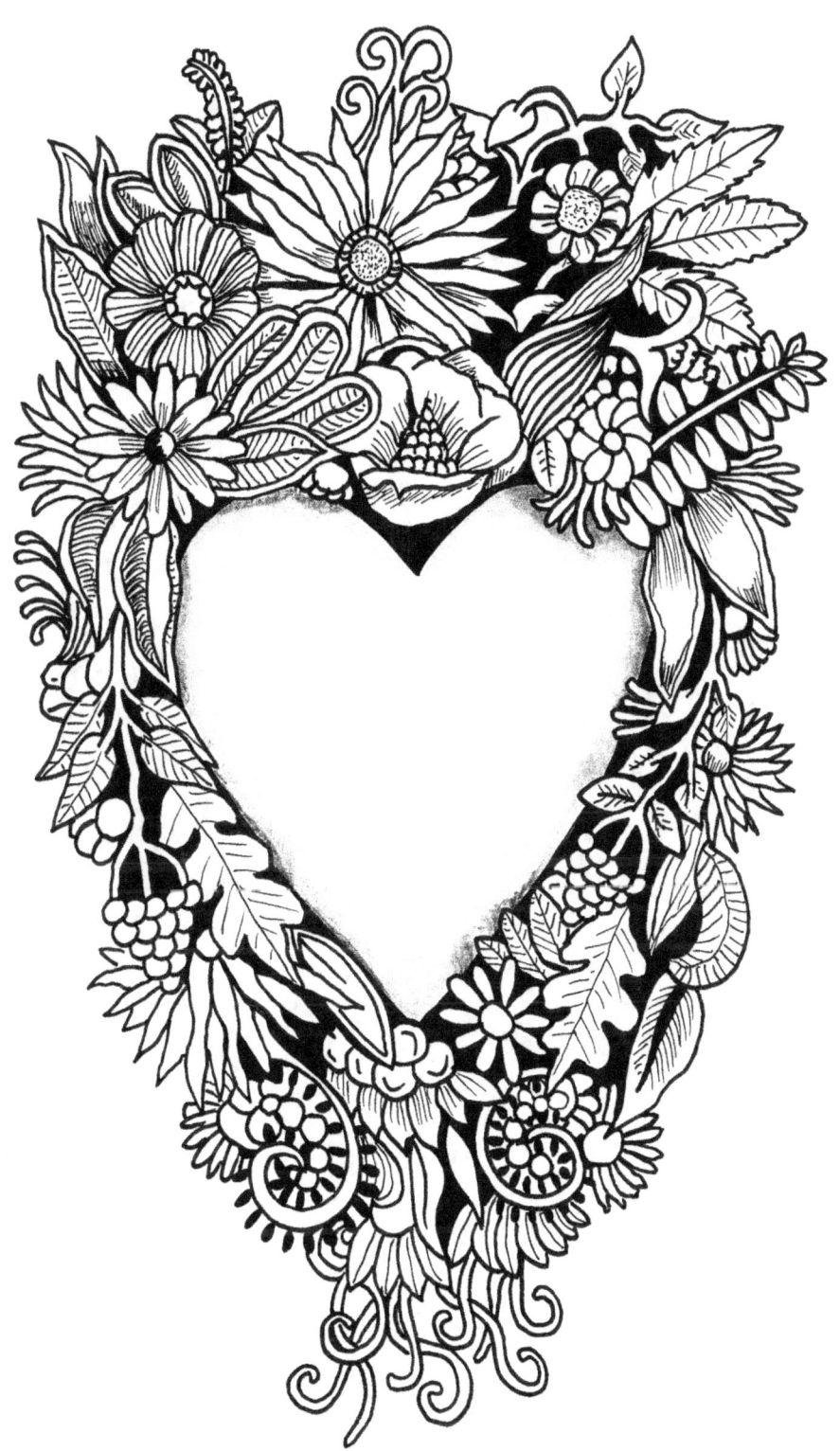

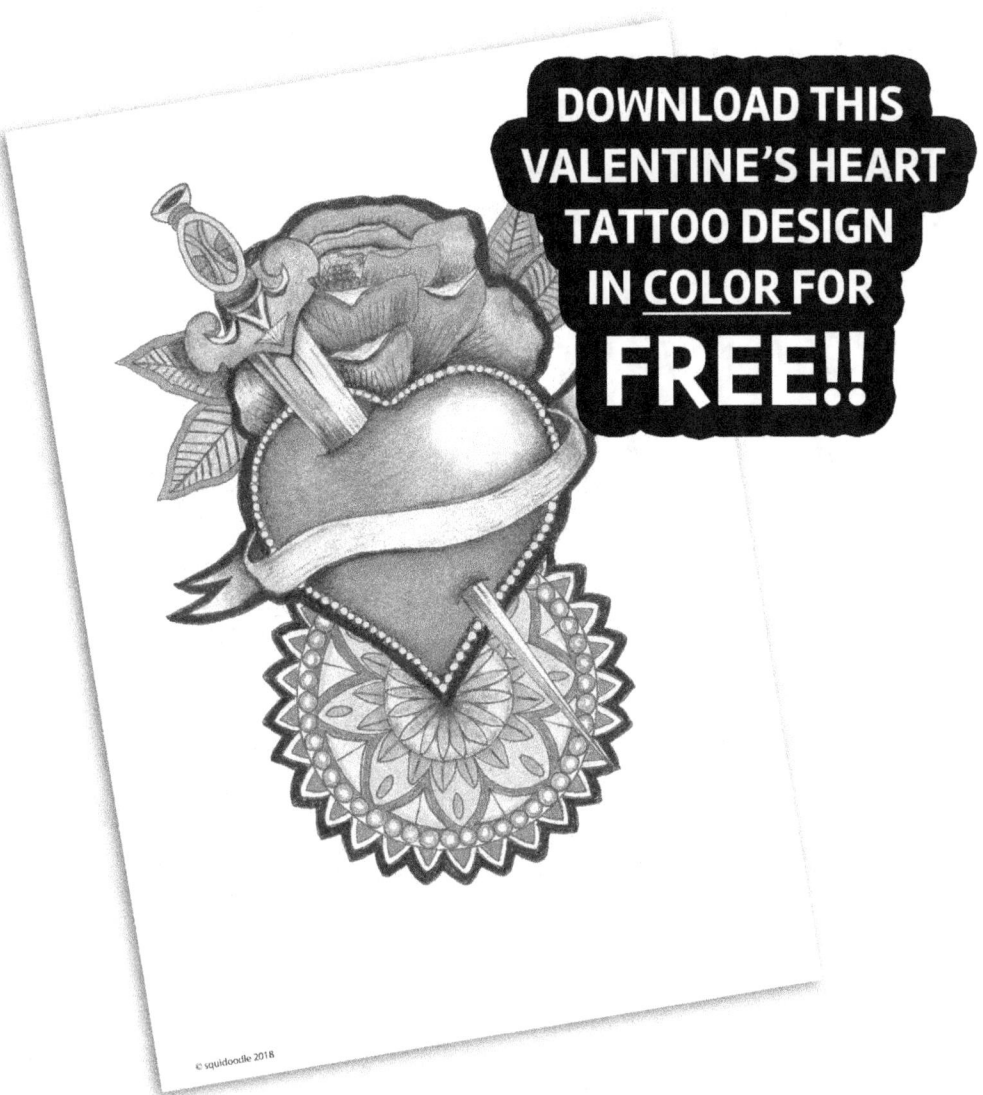

DOWNLOAD THIS VALENTINE'S HEART TATTOO DESIGN IN COLOR FOR FREE!!

© squidoodle 2018

Did you see this colored design on the back page of the book you are holding? You can download it for free on my website!!

Step 1: Log on to **www.squidoodleshop.com** and visit the freebies section.
Step 2: Click on the file named Valentine's Heart.
Step 3: Enter the password **dagger** to unlock it.
Step 4: Print the design on card or colored paper of your choice.
Step 5: Customize the scroll with the name of your choice.
Step 6: Frame it or make it into a card – done!

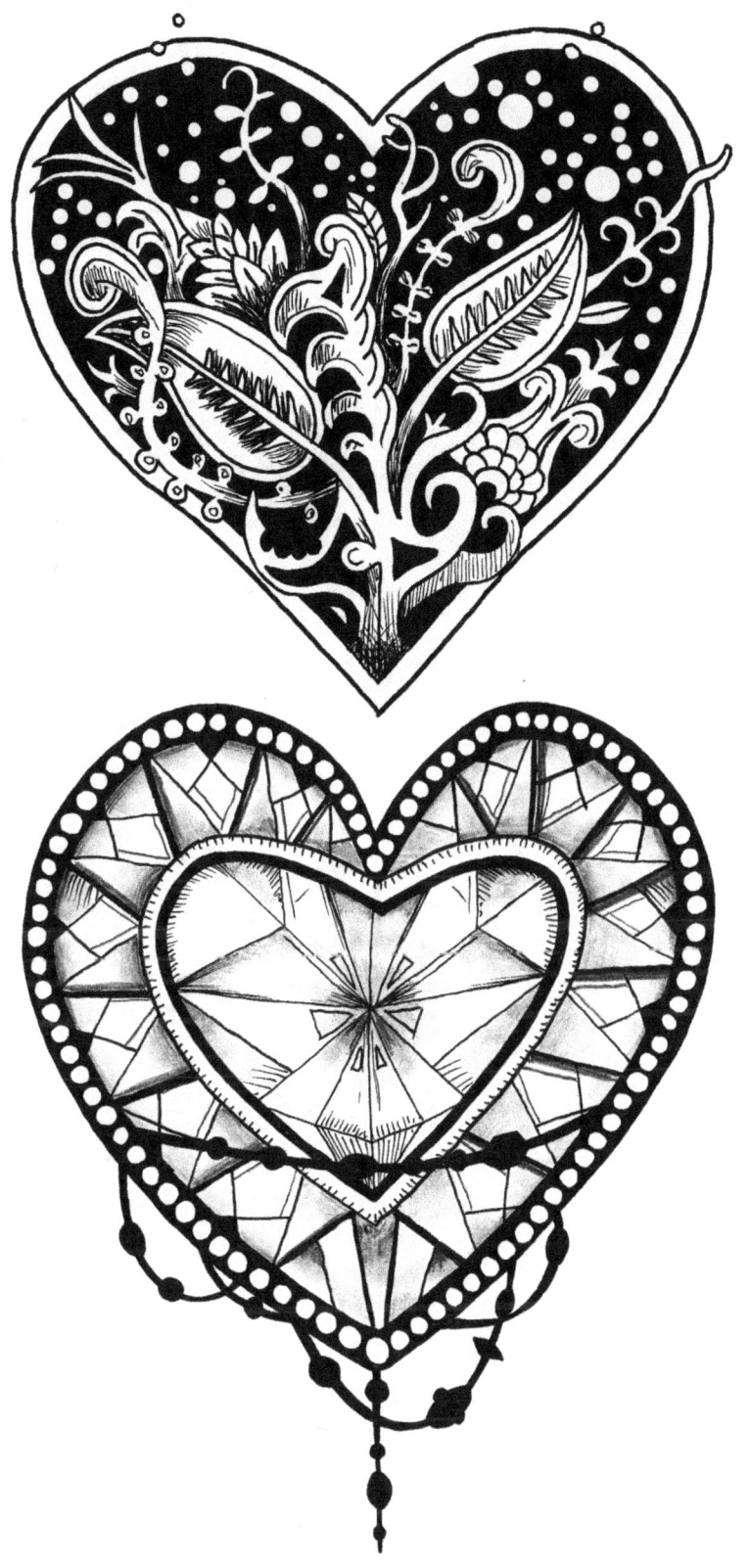

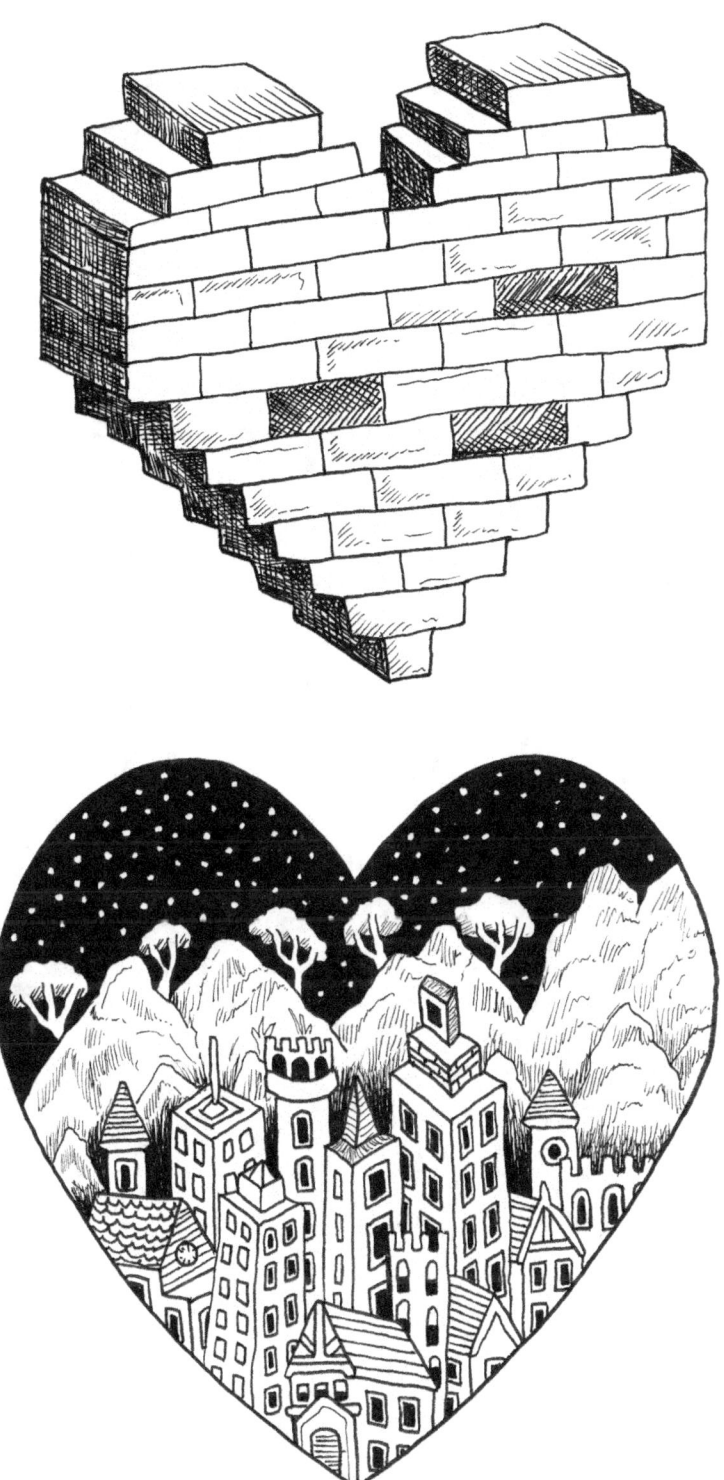

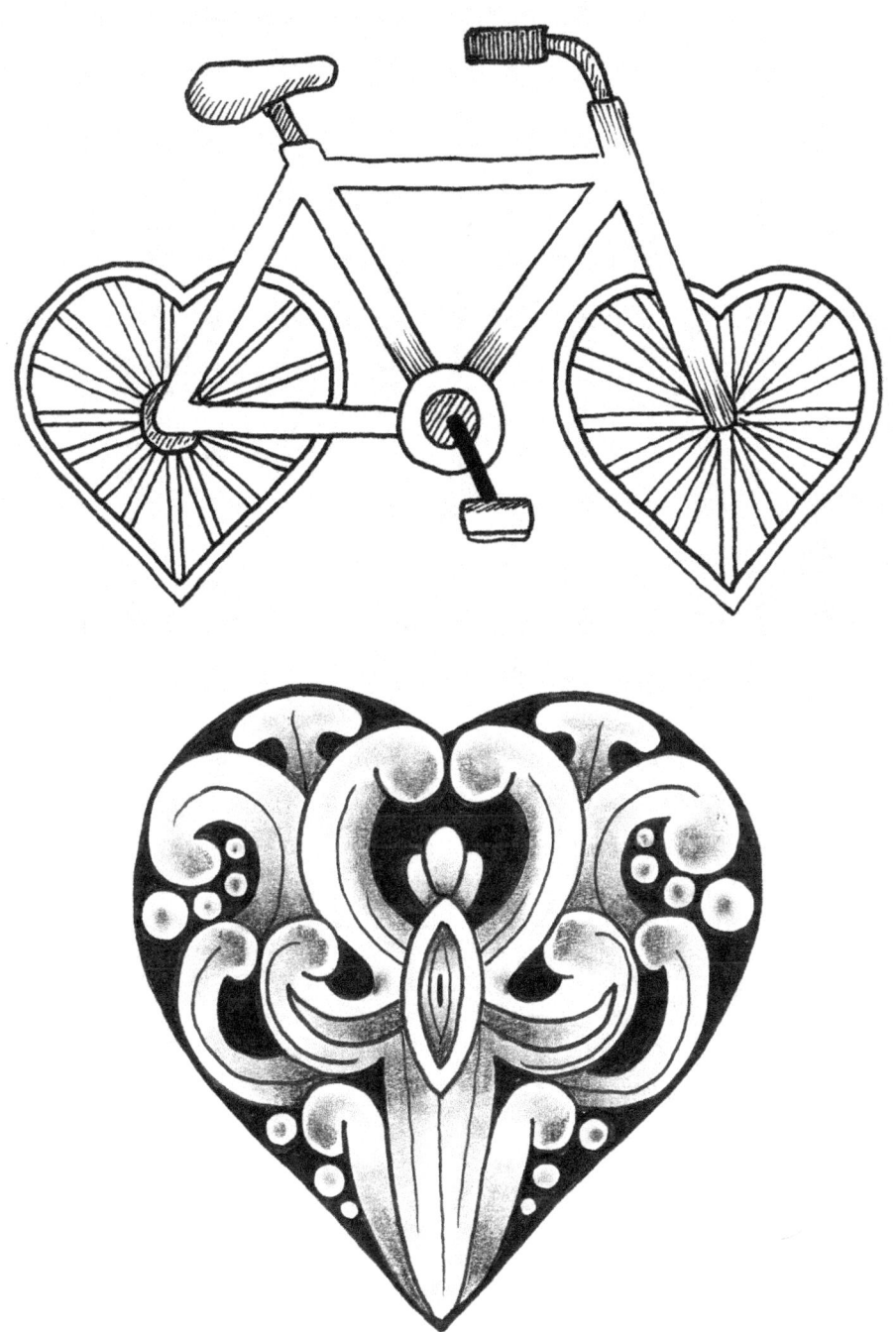

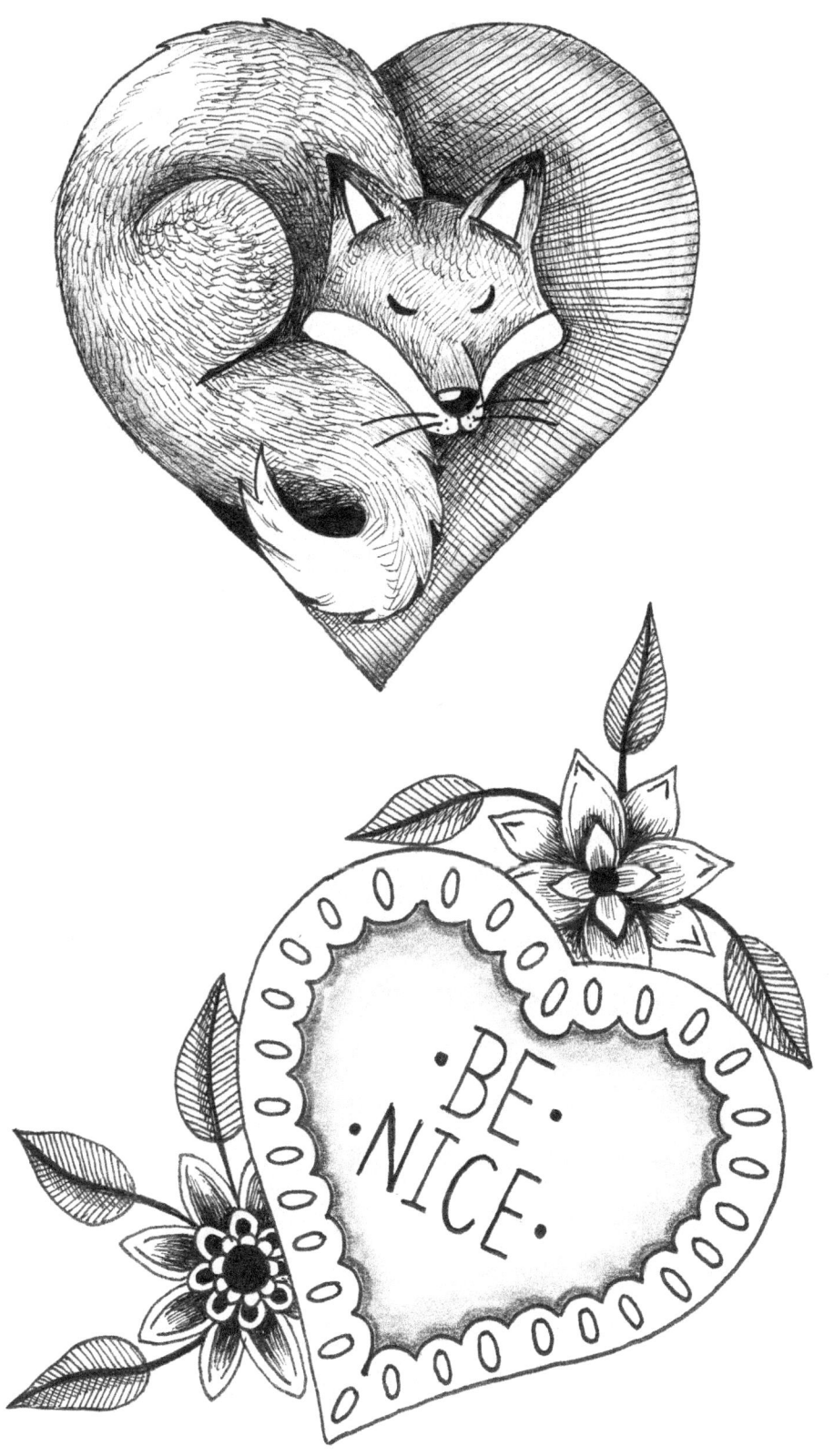

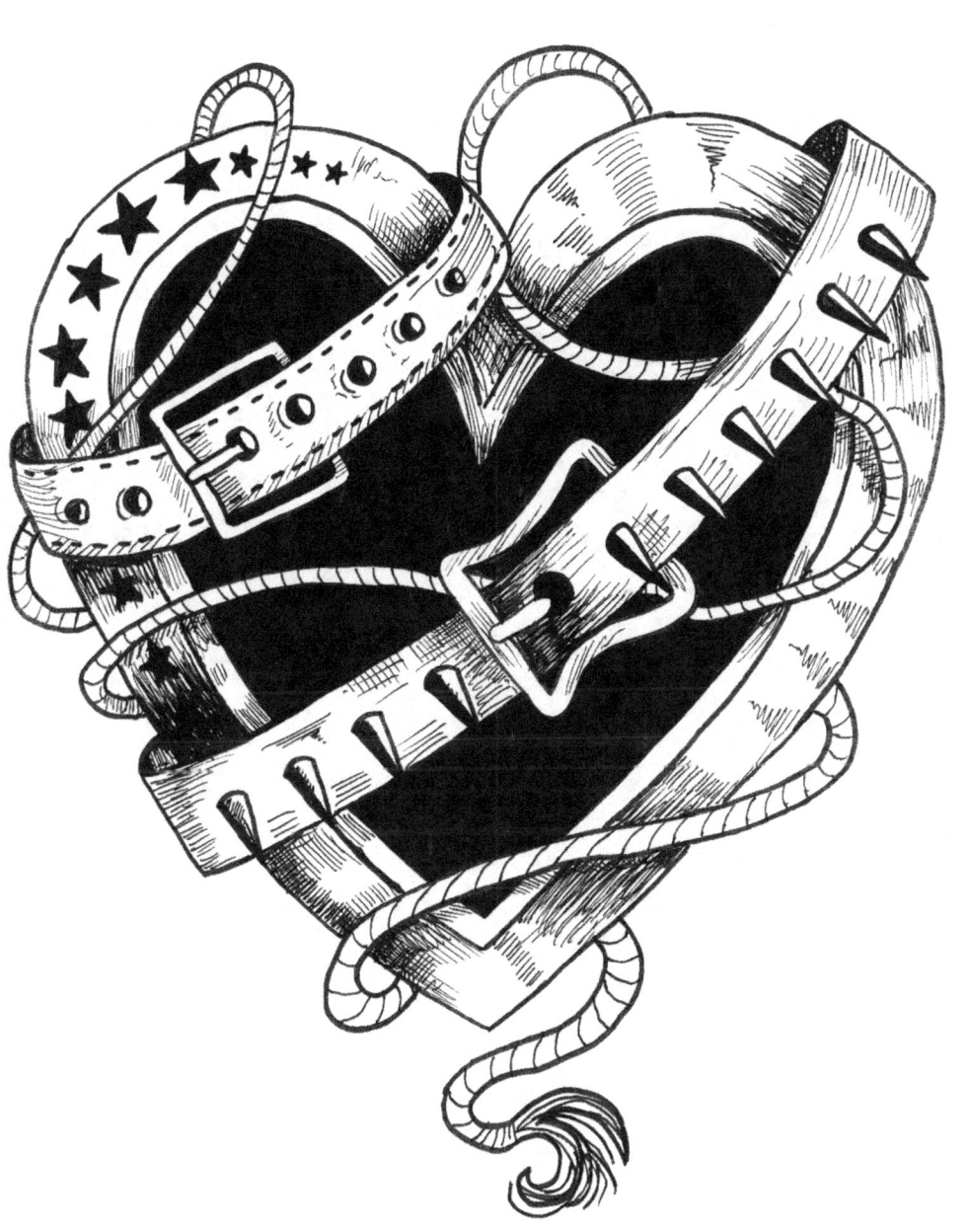

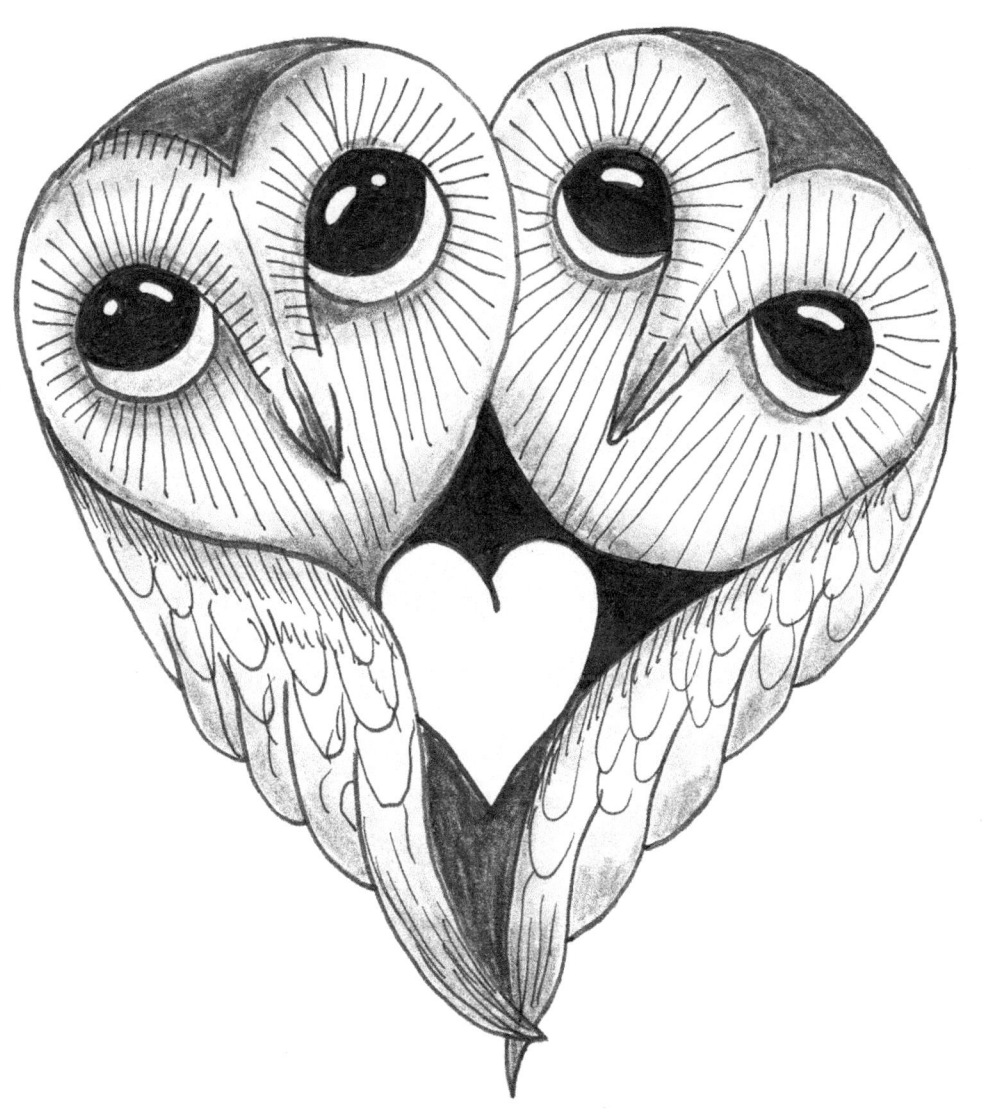

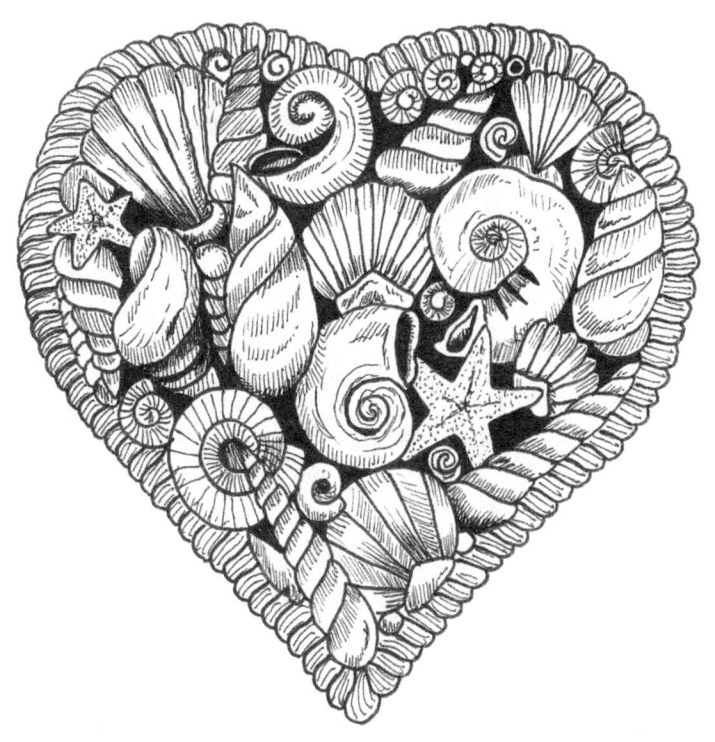

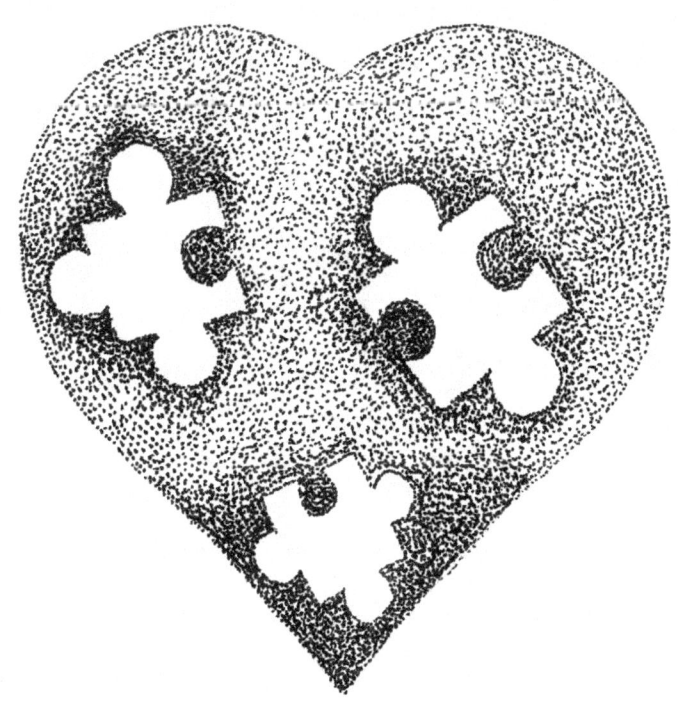

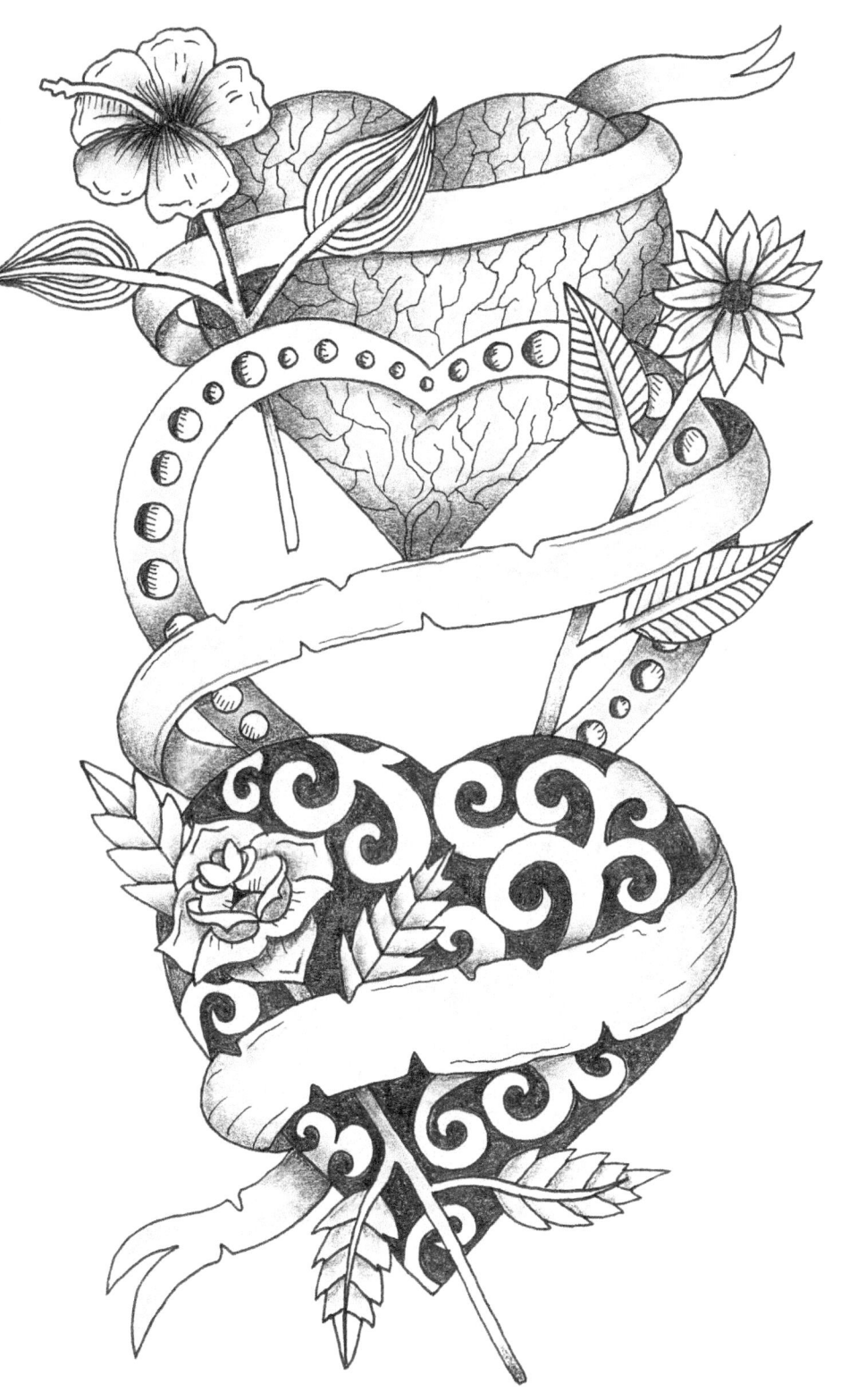

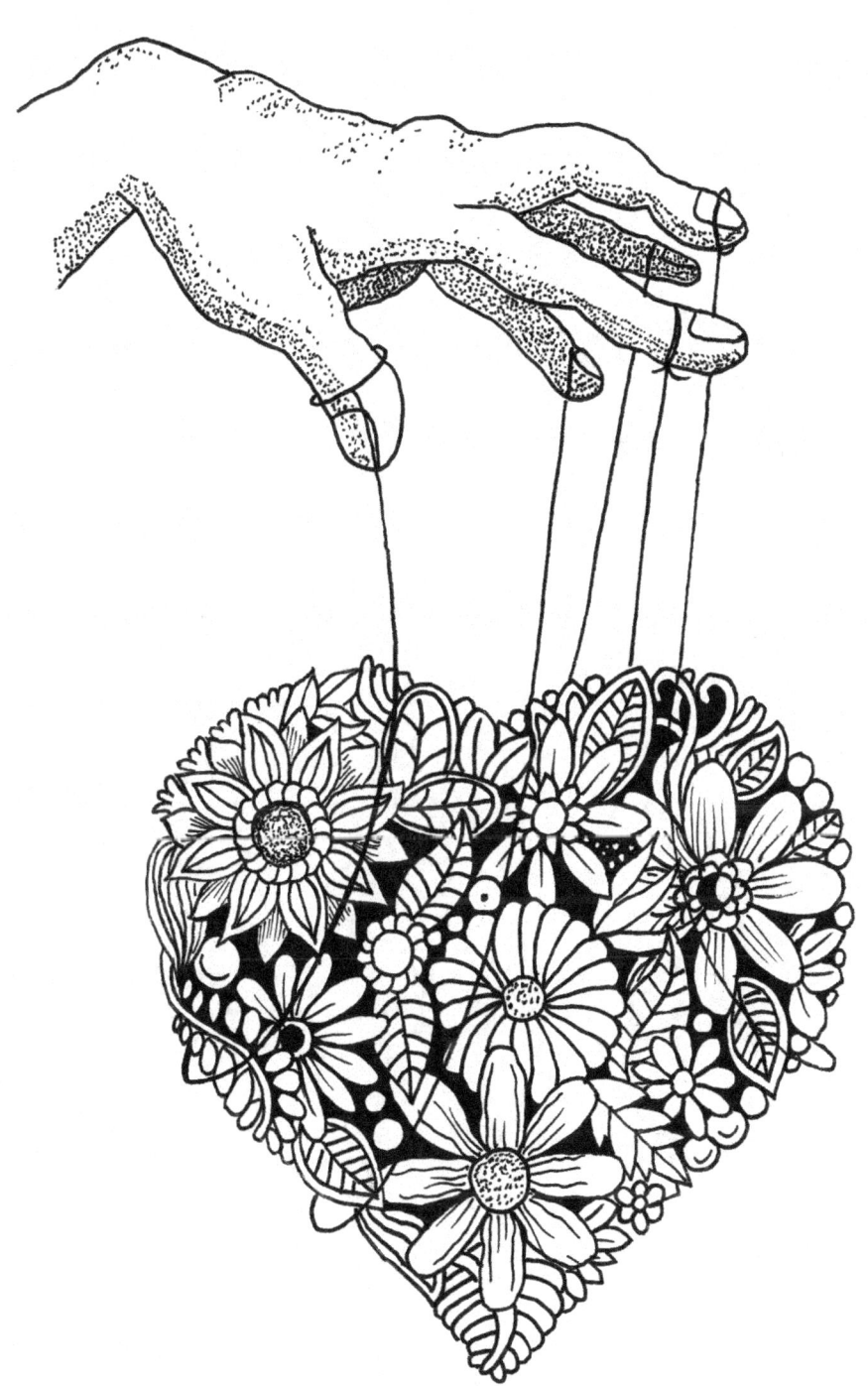

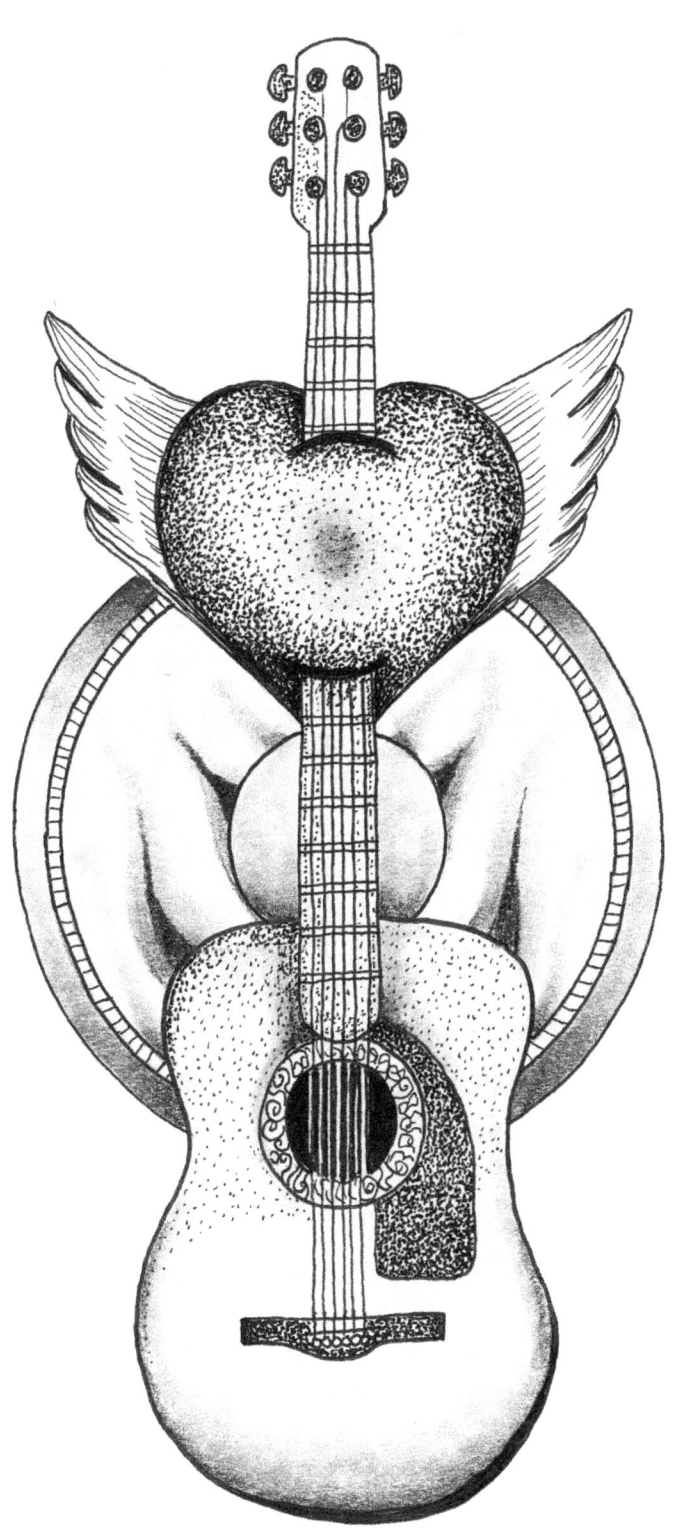

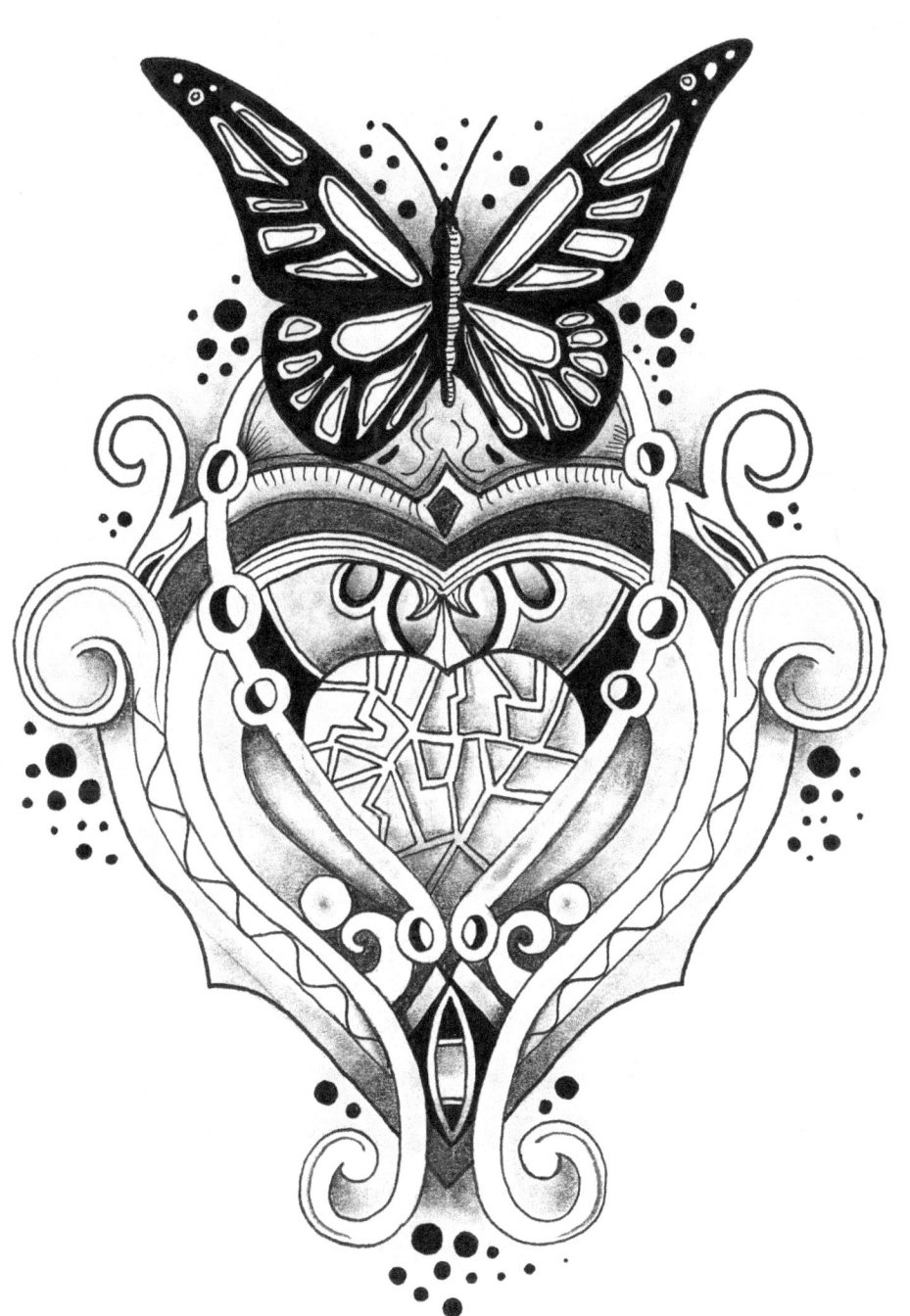

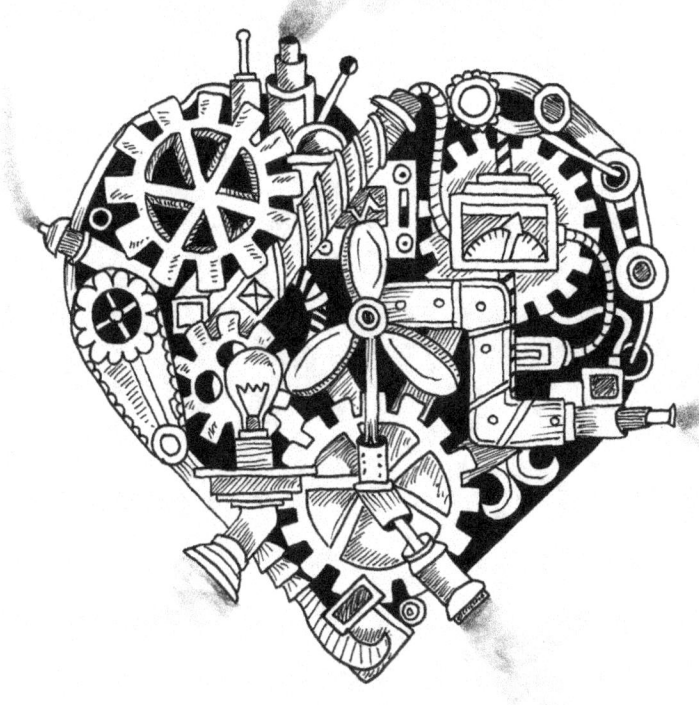

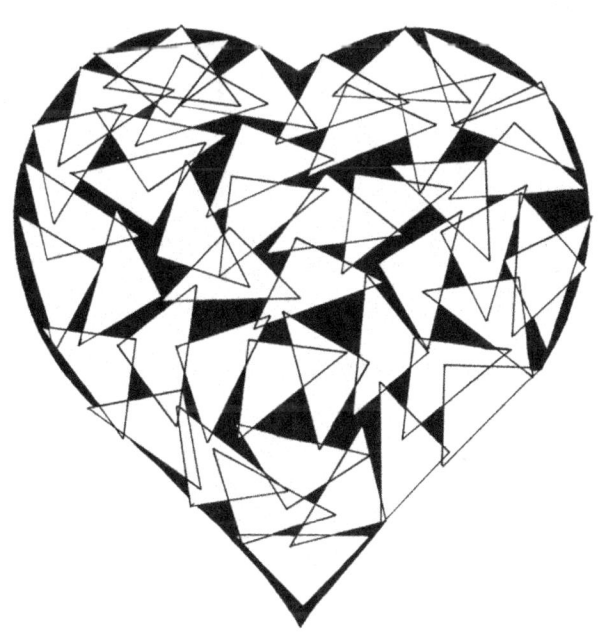

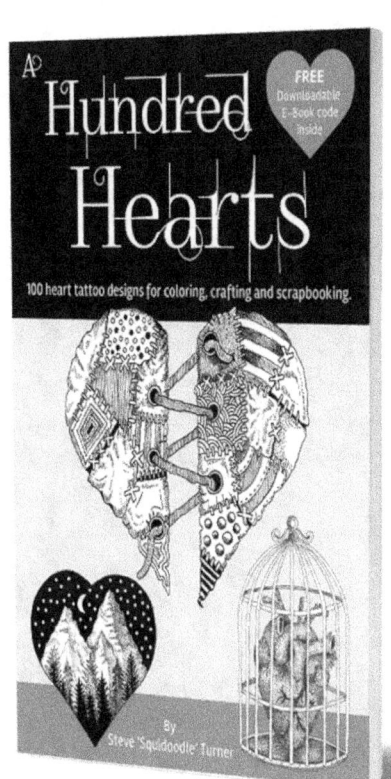

FREE
E-BOOK
DOWNLOAD!

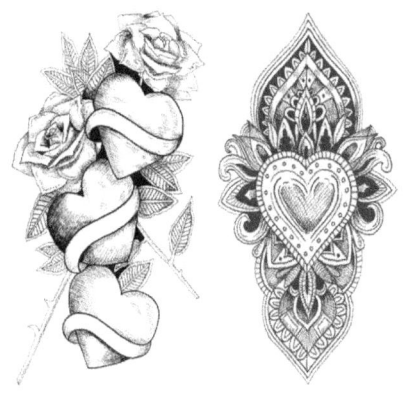

Enjoyed this book?
The fun doesn't stop here...

So you've cut the book up.... you've colored some of the hearts.... you've removed some for other projects... wanna do some more? As a special thank you for purchasing this book you can dowload EVERY SINGLE DESIGN on my website!

Simply visit **www.squidoodleshop.com** and click on the freebies section. You'll find a file there called Hundred Hearts E-Book. Download the file using the password **myhundredhearts** .....and print as many times as you like!

Support independent artists! This free download is only available to you as the buyer of the book. Please please please don't share the password... encourage people to buy the book instead!

...other Squidoodle coloring books available

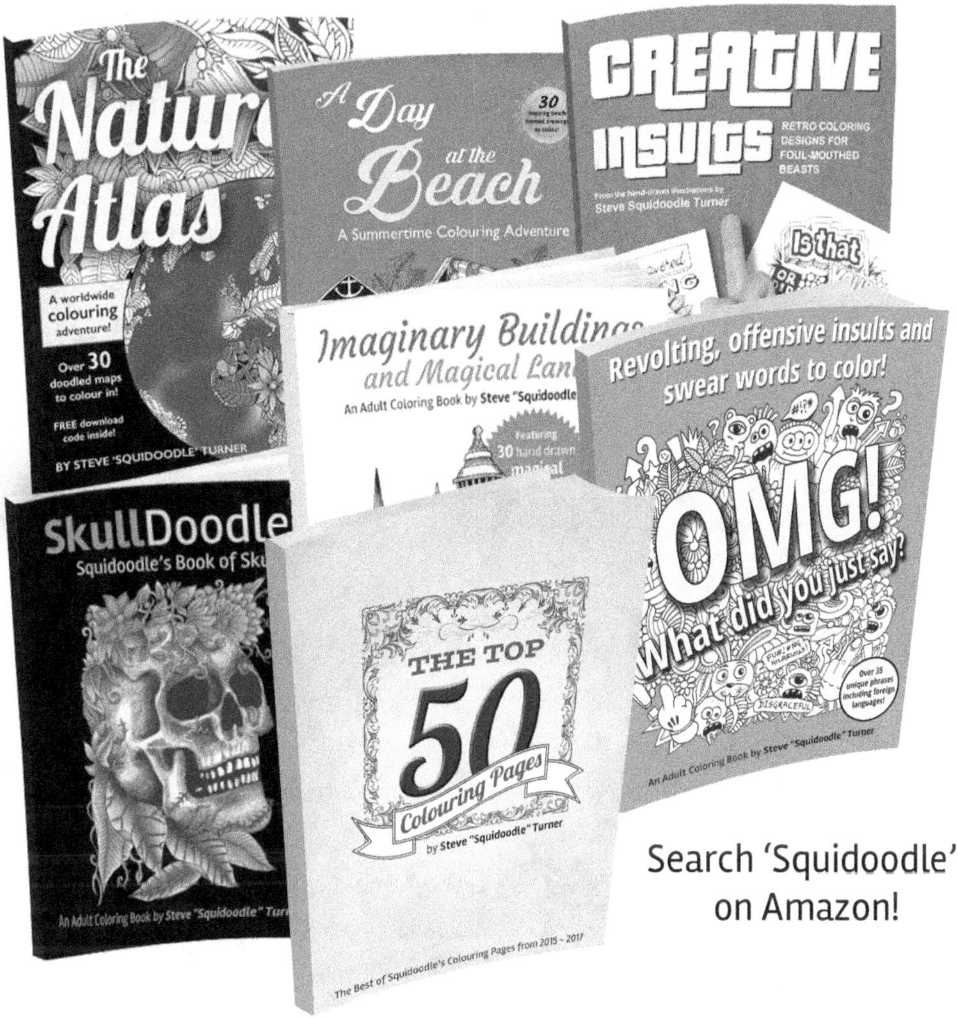

Search 'Squidoodle' on Amazon!

 @squidoodleart

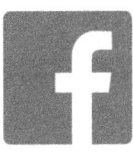 facebook.com/SquidDoodleArt

Make sure you follow me on instagram and facebook for regular giveaways and new book announcements!

www.ingramcontent.com/pod-product-compliance
Lightning Source LLC
Chambersburg PA
CBHW071315220526
45468CB00001B/387